INDENTURE TRUSTEE
Bankruptcy Powers & Duties

INDENTURE TRUSTEE
Bankruptcy Powers & Duties

By Stephanie Wickouski

Beard Books
Washington, D.C.

ISBN 1-58798-305-2

ABA Revised Simplified Model Indenture (2000).

Printed in the United States of America

This book is intended as a practical resource for indenture trustees, lawyers, advisors and professionals in the areas of restructuring and corporate trust. Its purpose is to provide useful information on the subject, and it is not intended by the publisher or author as legal, accounting or other professional advice or service.

To Harvey R. Miller
1933–2015

PREFACE

Harvey Miller, the most prominent bankruptcy lawyer in American history, died about the time I started writing this book.

Harvey was not a fan of indenture trustees, which has led some of my colleagues to question why I dedicate this book to him. While Harvey was not a mentor of mine, he influenced my path in bankruptcy law in ways I can't begin to list. He had a huge part in creating the industry which is my lifelong career and that of many readers of this book.

When my first book, *Bankruptcy Crimes*, was ready to be released, I asked Harvey to write an endorsement. Not only did he oblige, he reviewed the manuscript and sent me a list of substantive corrections. He also made the following comment:

> I do not agree that high profile bankruptcy cases have destroyed public confidence in the bankruptcy system, as stated in the overview. Bankruptcy continues to be an option for distressed business entities. I agree it is important to root out bankruptcy abuse. Those cases are a small percentage of the bankruptcy cases filed.

As his email reflects, Harvey was a true believer in the bankruptcy system. That system in turn was shaped by his beliefs.

Harvey's ideas changed the very nature of bankruptcy practice. He influenced me to lead the field forward with action and ideas.

When I wrote *Bankruptcy Crimes*, the law governing bankruptcy crime was underdeveloped and at a critical juncture. I wanted to have a hand in its evolution and direction.

Unlike the subject of my first book, the law pertaining to indenture trustees is well developed. The law, however, has not kept pace with the evolution of the capital markets industry.

INDENTURE TRUSTEE Bankruptcy Powers & Duties demystifies the legal role of the indenture trustee and offers practical, real-world tips, paving the way for enhanced trustee – bondholder communications, greater efficiency and enhanced recovery.

The restructuring and distressed investing industry travels at warp speed. With every new case comes new "technologies" — strategies used by debtors, investors, and third parties to maximize their return and opportunities. Every new technology brings a new set of questions and dilemmas for indenture trustees and investors.

While litigation between issuers and investors (and indenture trustees on their behalf) was once the exception, it is now the rule, bringing with it a pressing need for communication, coordination, and strategy.

Trustees and investors often find themselves in uncharted territory. This book is not a world map. It's more like a mobile phone app — a compass and level tool — providing direction and uniformity, ultimately guiding users to their desired destinations.

ACKNOWLEDGMENTS

Many people inspired me to write this book and I am grateful to all of them.

First and foremost, my terrific clients: indenture trustees, distressed investors, hedge funds, and other debt security holders who educated me about their industries.

Next, my great editor and publisher, Nina Novak and Beard Books, who collaborated with me on my first book, *Bankruptcy Crimes*. I could not have written this book without them.

My husband, David Fletcher, who responded to the avalanche of paper which accompanies the writing of a book with an abundance of humor and encouragement. Also, my sister, Sheila Wickouski, herself a published author, who first taught me to write and helped me with advice along the way.

My law firm Bryan Cave LLP for enthusiastic and unfailing support for my undertaking this project. Special thanks to my colleagues Jeremy Finkelstein, Jeannette Lugo, Howard Rogatnick, and Gail Young.

Thanks to Harold Kaplan, who is the source of many ideas that are memorialized in this book, as well as a good friend.

Last and not least, praise to my revered committee — Anthony, Therese and JT — who responded to my every request, no matter how difficult, ordinary, or hopeless.

TERMS AND ABBREVIATIONS

ABA	American Bar Association
Bankruptcy Code	Title 11, United States Code §§ 101–1532
bankruptcy court	A unit of the district court in each federal judicial district, composed of the bankruptcy judges in regular active service, established under 28 U.S.C. § 151
Committee	An official committee of unsecured creditors appointed under 11 U.S.C. § 1102
DTC	The Depository Trust Company
Fed. R. Bankr. P.	Federal Rules of Bankruptcy Procedure
LENS	DTC's Legal Notice System
Model Indenture	American Bar Association Revised Simplified Model Indenture and Commentary, 53 Bus. Law 1115 (2000)
PACER	Public Access to Court Electronic Records, a centralized, electronic, publicly available service through which judicial court documents can be obtained
Securities Act	Securities Act of 1933 (15 U.S.C. §§ 77a–aa, as amended)
SPR	Securities Position Report
TIA	Trust Indenture Act of 1939 (15 U.S.C. §§ 77aaa-bbbb, as amended)

ABOUT THE AUTHOR

Stephanie Wickouski is an American bankruptcy lawyer. A partner with the New York City office of Bryan Cave LLP, she has practiced bankruptcy law for more than 35 years, litigating complex reorganization cases throughout the country and serving as lead bankruptcy counsel in multiple high-profile cases, including *Energy Future, Caesars Entertainment, United Airlines, Northwest Airlines, General Maritime, General Motors, Hayes Lemmerz, ION Media, Escada, Bally Total Fitness, Dex Media, New Page, Independence Air, Loral Orion, USGen New England, Tower Automotive, WHX Corp., Armstrong World Industries,* and *Friendly Restaurants.*

Named in *New York Super Lawyers* and *The Best Lawyers in America* year after year, she is a well known presence in the national bankruptcy community. She has been named as one of the 12 Outstanding Restructuring Lawyers in the U.S. by *Turnarounds & Workouts.* She is the author of *Bankruptcy Crimes* (3rd Ed.) (Beard Books), the leading authoritative treatise on bankruptcy crime, and the *Corporate Restructuring Blog* (http://blogs.bankrupt.com/).

Stephanie Wickouski can be reached at stephanie.wickouski@bryancave.com or info@indenturetrustee.nyc.

CONTENTS

PAGE

PART 1

INTRODUCTION

PART 1:

Introduction

Chapter 1. Debt Securities and the Indenture Trustee

1.1 What is an indenture trustee?

A person (usually a bank, financial institution, trust company, and/or national association) designated with specific rights, powers, and duties under an indenture.

1.2 What is an indenture?

An indenture is an agreement under which debt securities are issued. The indenture governs the terms of a debt security (such as a note, bond, or debenture). It is the instrument used to effectuate the issuance of debt securities.

The indenture contains the terms of the debt security, including: the maximum principal amount of securities that can be issued under the indenture, interest rate, interest payment dates, record dates, maturity date, representations, covenants, defaults, and remedies.

1.3 What is a debt security?

A form of debt instrument in which a company, municipality or other institution borrows funds by issuing debt securities, which are payable with a defined term and interest rate. Most corporate debt securities are fixed income securities and are traded on public exchanges or over-the-counter.

1.4 What are the types of debt securities?

There are three main types: (1) corporate, (2) municipal, and (3) United States Treasury. Corporate and municipal bonds are issued under an indenture, which requires an indenture trustee. Municipal securities (and the indentures and other documents under which they are issued) are distinct in several respects from corporate debt securities. Municipal securities are discussed in Chapter 2.

1.5 What is the difference between a note, a bond, and a debenture?

"Notes" commonly mean debt instruments of an intermediate term, between one and ten years.

"Bonds" are secured obligations having a term of more than ten years.

"Debentures" generally refer to unsecured obligations having a term of more than ten years, *i.e.,* unsecured bonds.

Despite these historical definitions, in current parlance, notes, bonds and debentures are all used interchangeably and are all commonly referred to as "bonds."

1.6 What are some basic terms used in connection with debt securities?

The issuance price of a bond is called "par." The actual price paid by investors for the security (*i.e.* its market price) may be higher or lower, depending on numerous factors, including the credit quality of the issuer, the interest rate relative to other investments, and the term.

The interest rate is often referred to as the "coupon rate" and the interest payments referred to as the "coupon." A typical coupon date schedule is quarterly, semi-annually, or annually.

"Maturity date" is the date on which all of the outstanding obligations under the debt securities must be paid in full. This includes the outstanding face value as well as any other obligations that have accrued or become due.

A common feature in modern corporate debt securities is to provide for interest-only payments over the term, with the entire principal amount to be paid at maturity. Some indentures contain provisions prohibiting the issuer from repaying or refinancing the securities prior to the maturity date (referred to as "no call" provisions). Other indentures provide that the issuer has the option to repay (or "redeem") the securities prior to the maturity date only with a payment of an additional amount to compensate holders for the lost interest over the remaining term. Such payment is referred to as a "make-whole" premium.

A "sinking fund" is a device for repayment and reduction of principal during the term of the debt security. This is not a common feature in corporate debt securities.

1.7 What is the function of debt securities in corporate finance?

Businesses need capital to operate. One source of raising capital which companies may use is the issuance of debt securities offered to investors in a public or private offering. Financing capital through the issuance of debt securities is an alternative to borrowing money from a bank.

Debt securities are issued by the offering party, which, in the case of corporate debt financing, is the obligor under the indenture.

1.8 Why is an independent indenture trustee required?

Following the stock market crash of 1929, Congress enacted a series of laws regulating the issuance, purchase, and sale of debt securities. One of these laws was the Trust Indenture Act of 1939, 15 U.S.C.

§§ 77aaa-77bbbb (the "TIA").[1] The TIA forbids the sale of notes, bonds, or debentures in interstate commerce unless the security has been issued under an indenture qualified under the TIA. There are a number of exceptions, including that debt securities issued in private placements are exempt from registration under section 4(a)(2) of the Securities Act of 1933, 15 U.S.C. §§ 77a-77aa.

The TIA requires the appointment of a qualified, independent, institutional indenture trustee in public debt offerings exceeding $10 million. In order to be independent, a trustee, among other things, must not be controlled by, or under common control with, an issuer or underwriter.

One of the primary reasons for the requirement of an independent trustee is to establish a means whereby the debt securities holders can enforce their rights collectively in a default or bankruptcy proceeding of the issuer. Where there are tens if not hundreds of holders, collective action by an indenture trustee provides the only practical and effective means for enforcement of remedies by holders.

In furtherance of ensuring independence on the part of the indenture trustees, the TIA requires the resignation and replacement of an indenture trustee upon the default of the issuer where certain events create a conflict of interest for the trustee. The TIA explicitly defines such conflicts. The most common conflicts arise where the same institution is the trustee under two or more tranches of securities with different priorities (*e.g.*, senior and subordinated, or secured and unsecured), or where the institution is also the underwriter or a lender.

1.9 What is the relationship between the Trust Indenture Act and an indenture?

The TIA specifies certain substantive provisions that must be included in every indenture governed by the TIA. These provisions are set forth in sections 310-317 of the TIA. While usually included in a qualified indenture, these provisions apply and are deemed included in the indenture whether the indenture expressly contains them or not. TIA § 318(c). Further, if the language in an indenture varies from that in the TIA, the TIA will control.

1.10 What is a TIA-qualified indenture?

If a debt issuance is subject to and not exempt from the TIA, the indenture must be qualified with the Securities and Exchange Commission (SEC) before sales of the securities can be made. TIA § 306. To be qualified, the indenture must be included with the issuer's registration statement filed with the SEC.

1.11 Are all indentures governed by the TIA?

No. Section 304 of the TIA delineates a number of exemptions to the applicability of the TIA. For example, equity securities are not included. The TIA exempts securities other than notes, bonds, debentures, or debt certificates. Issuances under $10 million in the aggregate are also exempt.

An indenture that is exempt from the TIA may provide by its terms that it nonetheless is governed by the TIA.

1.12 What is the role of the indenture trustee under indentures governed by the TIA?

Section 315(a)(1) of the TIA provides that, prior to a default, the trustee shall not be liable except for the performance of duties as specifically set out in the indenture. The provision is explicitly incorporated into most modern indentures.

As long as a default has not occurred under the indenture, the duties and role of the indenture trustee are purely administrative or agency functions, such as the receipt of quarterly and annual reports. The pre-default role of the indenture trustee does not bear any resemblance to the role of a trustee under common law.

The indenture trustee may also serve as registrar, transfer agent, paying agent, and/or conversion agent, as applicable.

1.13 Besides the TIA and federal securities laws, what other laws govern the interpretation of indentures?

Except where preempted by federal law, state law will apply to the interpretation of an indenture. Under the Supremacy Clause of the United States Constitution, *U.S. Const. art. VI, cl. 3,* state laws that interfere with, or are contrary to, federal law, are invalid. Preemption arises where an actual conflict exists between federal and state law and the state law stands as an obstacle to the accomplishment and execution of the full purposes and objectives of Congress. *See Crosby v. Nat'l Foreign Trade Council,* 530 U.S. 363, 372-73 (2000).

Accordingly, state law will apply to the interpretation of an indenture, to the extent the question is not implicated by the TIA. Most corporate indentures contain broad choice of law provisions which agree both as to a choice of governing law and jurisdiction in a particular forum. The choice of governing law is usually New York law. Some typical language is:

> The Indenture and the Securities shall be governed by, and construed in accordance with, the laws of the State of New York. The Issuer consents to the jurisdiction of the courts of the State of New York and any federal court, in each case located in the borough of Manhattan in New York City.

1.14 Have courts generally upheld choice of law provisions in indentures?

Yes. Choice of law provisions are respected where the chosen law has a reasonable relationship to the parties to the contract or the transaction at issue. *Welsbach Elec. Corp. v. MasTec N. Am., Inc.,*

7 N.Y.3d 624, 629, 825 N.Y.S.2d 692, 694 (2006).[2] The issue has been frequently considered by New York courts. Because many parties involved in a debt securities issuance have a nexus to New York, the choice of law provisions have generally been upheld. *See, e.g.*, *Ellington Credit Fund, Ltd. v. Select Portfolio Servicing, Inc.*, 837 F. Supp. 2d 162, 180 (S.D.N.Y. 2011); *Excelsior Fund, Inc. v. JP Morgan Chase Bank, N.A.*, 06 Civ. 5246(JGK), 2007 U.S. Dist. LEXIS 22966, at *16 (S.D.N.Y. Mar. 22, 2007); *see also* N.Y. Gen. Oblig. § 5-1401.

1.15 What is the "Model Indenture"?

In 1983, a form of indenture was developed by a subcommittee of the Section of Business Law of the American Bar Association, and was revised in 2000.[3] The ABA Revised Simplified Model Indenture and Commentary, 53 BUS. LAW 1115 (2000)(the "Model Indenture"), was intended to create uniformity and streamline negotiations over indenture provisions. The Model Indenture includes numerous provisions of the TIA which are required in TIA qualified indentures.

Not all indentures follow the Model Indenture. There is considerable variance in the marketplace and specific refinements are often made by counsel on a case-by-case basis. In this book, references are made from time to time to the Model Indenture or to a typical indenture. In a given situation, however, the applicable indenture must be carefully examined, as it will be the governing document in that specific case.

1.16 How can the modern corporate trust industry in the United States be described?

The business of serving as an indenture trustee is a mature industry. Both the law and best practices are fairly well defined, although both continue to evolve, sometimes very rapidly.

The corporate trust industry is primarily dominated by a number of institutions including BNY Mellon, BOKF, ComputerShare Trust

Company, Delaware Trust Company, Deutsche Bank, HSBC Bank USA, Law Debenture Trust Company, MUFG Union Bank, Regions Bank, UMB, U.S. Bank, Wells Fargo, Wilmington Savings Fund Society, Wilmington Trust Company, and Zions Bank.

Chapter 2. Municipal Bonds

2.1 What are municipal bonds?

Municipal bonds are debt securities issued by a state or local government or agency. Municipal bond issuers include states, cities, counties, redevelopment agencies, authorities (such as housing, education or health), public utility districts, and airports.

There are three types of municipal bonds: general obligation bonds, revenue bonds, and conduit bonds. General obligation bonds are a direct obligation of the municipal issuer. Revenue bonds are non-recourse borrowings of a municipal entity that are repaid only from specific revenues. Conduit bonds are issued for the benefit of a non-governmental entity, such as a hospital, school, or utility. The latter arrangement is referred to as conduit financing because the municipal entity is merely a conduit or pass-through for the issuance of the bonds and is not responsible for their repayment.

Unlike general obligation bonds, revenue bonds and conduit bonds are not backed by the full faith and credit of the municipality.

2.2 What are some different types of revenue bonds?

There are many different types of revenue bonds, including airport revenue bonds, public power revenue bonds, highway revenue bonds, toll road revenue bonds, and industrial revenue bonds, to name only a few.

2.3 For what purposes are revenue bonds issued?

Revenue bonds are issued for a specific project, and the revenues generated by the project are intended to repay the bonds. Such projects may include schools, water and sewer systems, public housing, municipal office buildings, or courthouses.

2.4 Where can the basic information regarding the structure of a municipal bond transaction be found?

The disclosure document (sometimes called the official statement or private placement memorandum) is a summary of information regarding a municipal bond offering. The disclosure document is analogous to an offering memorandum or a prospectus for a corporate securities offering. While the disclosure document is not binding as to the terms of the bonds — the indenture and related operative documents are controlling — the underwriter is required to provide all material information to potential purchasers of the bonds.

2.5 How does the structure of conduit financing differ from corporate debt securities?

The structure of municipal bonds differs from corporate debt securities in a number of ways. The most basic structural difference is that the issuer of securities under the indenture is the municipal issuer, not the obligor. The proceeds of the bond issuance are lent to the obligor by the municipal issuer, the obligations of the issuer are assumed by the obligor, and the rights of the issuer against the obligor are assigned to the indenture trustee.

Municipal bond structures can vary widely from state to state. Municipal bond issuance is a product of state and local law, and the laws and regulations can vary widely jurisdiction to jurisdiction.

2.6 What are the purposes for which conduit bonds are issued?

Conduit bonds are issued through a municipality for a private activity, often conducted by a non-profit corporation. Some typical examples of projects funded by conduit bonds are hospitals, universities, low-income housing and industrial development.

Some conduit bonds take the form of installment sale and leaseback transactions, facility leases, or other financing variations.

2.7 What is credit enhancement?

Credit enhancement refers to bond insurance, letters of credit, or liquidity facilities which are obtained by an issuer to improve the credit rating of a bond. This is done in order to reduce the cost of the bond financing to the obligor.

Following an event of default in connection with a municipal bond backed by a letter of credit, the indenture trustee will usually be required under the bond documents to draw on the letter of credit prior to the expiration date of the letter of credit. In the case of insured municipal bonds, following an event of default, the insurer becomes the holder under the indenture with the right to direct the indenture trustee.

2.8 What is a debt service reserve?

A debt service reserve is an account held by the trustee under a municipal bond indenture which may be used to pay debt service if the obligor fails to meet its debt service obligations. A debt service reserve is often established from the proceeds of a debt securities issuance but in some municipal financings it is funded subsequently, or a letter of credit is provided instead of a debt service reserve.

When a debt service reserve is drawn upon to pay debt service, the obligor is typically required under the indenture to replenish the amount drawn.

A debt service reserve is distinct from a debt service fund, which is an account funded periodically by an obligor to pay debt service.

2.9 How are debt service reserves and other bond reserve funds affected by a bankruptcy filing of an obligor?

The use of and entitlement to debt service reserves, debt service funds, and other bond reserve funds created under an indenture and held by the trustee are often the subject of dispute in a bankruptcy case.

Debtors generally assert that bond reserve funds are property of the estate and/or cash collateral, and that the exercise of rights or remedies against such funds are subject to the automatic stay. Indenture trustees generally assert that the bond funds are property of the trustee which are held in trust for the holders, subject only to the charging lien rights of the indenture trustee. After an event of default, the issuer's interest in the funds is, at most, a reversionary interest in the event the bond obligations are paid in full.

Both of these characterizations are technically correct and, in fact, not inconsistent.

2.10 Do bond funds belong to the debtor or to the indenture trustee and the holders?

Bankruptcy courts have almost always viewed bond reserve funds as property of the indenture trustee held in trust on behalf of the holders, subject to any reversionary interest of the debtor. Property of the estate under Bankruptcy Code § 541 includes all interests of the debtor in property. Therefore, the property of the estate includes only any reversionary interest of the debtor in a bond reserve fund, not the bond reserve fund itself. *In re Central Medical Center, Inc.*, 122 B.R. 568 (Bankr. E.D. Mo. 1990).

2.11 May the indenture trustee draw down on bond reserve funds without first seeking relief from the automatic stay?

Whether drawing down on a bond reserve fund violates the automatic stay is a grey area. Indenture trustees as a rule have chosen not to test the question but instead to obtain relief from the stay, or a declaration that the stay is inapplicable, before drawing down on a bond reserve fund. Typically an agreement can be reached with the debtor to permit the trustee to withdraw funds from a reserve — usually to pay fees and expenses, and sometimes to distribute interest to holders — subject to the debtor's reservation of rights with respect to the allocation of the funds under a plan. This means that the debtor in its plan can allocate or credit amounts that have been used by the indenture trustee for fees, expenses, or interest, against the outstanding principal or in some other manner against the outstanding obligation.

Chapter 3. The Post-Default Indenture Trustee

3.1 Which indenture provisions are most significant when the issuer has defaulted in its obligations or filed for bankruptcy?

Virtually any provision of an indenture can be significant in a given case. The indenture provisions that are implicated most in a bankruptcy are the provisions governing payment terms, the rights of the indenture trustee and the holders, the powers and duties of the indenture trustee, events of default, remedies, and compensation and indemnification.

3.2 Why are provisions governing payment terms significant in a bankruptcy case?

Payment term provisions govern the entitlement to principal and interest (including additional interest and default interest), and the calculation of interest. Payment terms will determine the calculation of the claim, and, therefore, are instructive to the indenture trustee in preparing the proof of claim to be filed and in calculating distributions to holders.

3.3 What are events of default?

Events of default are events defined under the indenture which trigger the indenture trustee's rights to enforce or to exercise remedies under the indenture.

Indentures often use both the defined term "Event of Default" as well as the term "default," which is sometimes undefined. A default is an event that is, or with the passage of time or the giving of notice, becoming an "Event of Default."

Typical events of default include:

- If the company fails to pay interest when due and payable, and such failure continues for thirty days.
- If the company fails to pay the principal when due upon the maturity date, redemption date, or otherwise.
- If the company fails to comply with any agreements under the securities or the indenture and such failure is not cured after notice.
- If the company files a voluntary bankruptcy case or is the subject of an involuntary bankruptcy case (or similar case under insolvency laws) which is not dismissed after thirty days.

See, *e.g.*, Model Indenture § 6.01 (Events of Default).

3.4 What are the rights and duties of the indenture trustee?

The indenture defines the rights and duties of the trustee. Prior to a default or an event of default, the indenture trustee's duties are only those specifically set forth in the indenture. This is established by statute in the case of TIA-qualified indentures. TIA section 315(a) provides in pertinent part:

> **Section 315. Duties Prior to Default**
>
> (a) The indenture to be qualified shall automatically be deemed (unless it is expressly provided therein that any such provision is excluded) to provide that, prior to default (as such term is defined in such indenture)
>
> (1) the indenture trustee shall not be liable except for the performance of such duties as are specifically set out in such indenture;
>
> (2) the indenture trustee may conclusively rely, as to the truth of the statements and the correctness of

> the opinions expressed therein, in the absence of bad faith on the part of such trustee, upon certificates or opinions conforming to the requirements of the indenture; but the indenture trustee shall examine the evidence furnished to it pursuant to section 314 to determine whether or not such evidence conforms to the requirements of the indenture.

TIA § 315(a).

The duties of the indenture trustee change upon an event of default. Following an event of default, the indenture trustee has increased duties, which are defined in the case of a TIA-qualified indenture by reference to the "prudent person" standard provided in section 315(c) of the TIA. The Model Indenture language tracks TIA § 315(c):

> If an Event of Default has occurred and is continuing, the Trustee shall exercise such of the rights and powers vested in it by this Indenture, and use the same degree of care and skill in their exercise, as a prudent person would exercise or use under the circumstances in the conduct of its own affairs.

Model Indenture § 7.01(a).

PRACTICE TIP

It is an open question as to whether the "prudent person" standard applies to a trustee under an indenture which is not governed by the TIA. Best practices for corporate indenture trustees indicate that the prudent person standard is assumed once an event of default has occurred, even in the case of a corporate indenture that is exempt from the TIA.

3.5 Is an indenture trustee a fiduciary?

This is one of the most controversial questions in the corporate trust industry. *See, e.g.*, Harold L. Kaplan & Mark F. Hebbeln, The Anglo-American Indenture—Covenant Enforcement and Bond Defaults—U.S. Experience and Lessons from Canada and the U.K., A.B.A. SEC. BUS. LAW 1, 4 (Spring 2009), available at: http://www.abanet.org/buslaw/newsletter/0081/materials/pp1.pdf; Steven L. Schwarcz, Fiduciaries with Conflicting Obligations, available at: http://scholarship.law.duke.edu/cgi/viewcontent.cgi?article=2757&context=faculty_scholarship.

The standard indenture by its terms does not expressly create a fiduciary relationship. From time to time, courts have addressed the question of whether the indenture trustee is a fiduciary or has fiduciary duties. Courts and commentators have largely rejected the notion that an indenture trustee is a fiduciary prior to an event of default.

It has been held that even prior to default the indenture trustee has a duty to perform ministerial acts in a non-negligent manner. *AG Capital Funding Partners, L.P. v. State St. Bank & Trust Co.*, 11 N.Y.3d 146, 157, 866 N.Y.S.2d 578, 584 (2008). Even so, this is not the same as a fiduciary duty. *In AG Capital Funding*, the court held "that an indenture trustee owes a duty to perform its ministerial functions with due care, and if this duty is breached the trustee will be subjected to tort liability. However,...breach of such duty [does not] give[] rise to fiduciary duties…." *Id.*

Despite the fact the indenture trustee is not a fiduciary prior to an event of default, the duties of the indenture trustee after an event of default (and specifically, the prudent person standard) have been regarded by many courts and commentators as akin to, or analogous to, a fiduciary duty in some respects. The prudent person standard requires a higher level of engagement than strictly contractual or ministerial duties.

In *BNP Paribas Mortg. Corp. v. Bank of America, N.A.*, 778 F. Supp. 2d 375 (S.D.N.Y. 2011), the United States District Court for the Southern District of New York wrote:

> After an event of default, the indenture trustee's fiduciary duties expand by operation of New York common law, *LNC Invs., Inc. v. First Fid. Bank, N.A.*, 935 F. Supp. 1333, 1347–48 (S.D.N.Y. 1996), such that "fidelity to the terms of an indenture does not immunize an indenture trustee against claims that the trustee has acted in a manner inconsistent with his or her fiduciary duty of undivided loyalty to trust beneficiaries," and "the indenture trustee's obligations come more closely to resemble those of an ordinary fiduciary, regardless of any limitations or exculpatory provisions contained in the indenture," *Beck*, 632 N.Y.S.2d at 520, 527-28.

778 F. Supp. 2d at 401.

A common factor between fiduciaries and indenture trustees is the duty to avoid conflicts of interest, although circumstances which give rise to a conflict are much more limited in the case of an indenture trustee.

3.6 Do holders have a right to sue an indenture trustee for failing to act as a prudent person?

Yes. In addition to a contractual right as a beneficiary under the indenture, holders may have a right to bring an action under the TIA. While the TIA does not expressly create a private right of action, several courts have inferred such a right. *Zeffiro v. First Pennsylvania Banking and Trust Co.*, 623 F.2d 290, 294-99 (3d Cir. 1980) (applying the test of *Cort v. Ash*, 422 U.S. 66 (1975), and concluding that a right of action may be inferred under § 315(c) of the TIA); *In re Equity Funding Corp. of Am. Sec. Litig.*, 416 F. Supp. 161, 203 (C.D. Cal. 1976) (adopting the approach of *Morris v. Cantor, infra*), *aff'd*, 603 F.2d 1353 (9th Cir. 1979); *Morris v. Cantor*, 390 F. Supp. 817, 822 (S.D.N.Y. 1975) (deriving right to sue from jurisdictional section of TIA); *see also Caplin v. Marine Midland Grace Trust Co. of N.Y.*, 406 U.S. 416, 426 n.17 (1972) (suggesting that the TIA creates a private right of action, but declining to decide the issue).

The rights created under section 315(c) of the TIA do not, however, create rights of contribution against third parties, such as the indenture trustee's professionals or agents.

3.7 Does the indenture provide limitations on the liability of the indenture trustee?

Yes, most indentures do exactly that. For example, the Model Indenture contains a number of limitations on the liability of the indenture trustee. Some frequently included provisions which limit or protect the indenture trustee include:

> In the absence of bad faith on its part, the Trustee may conclusively rely, as to the truth of the statements and the correctness of the opinions expressed therein, upon certificates and opinions furnished to the Trustee and conforming to the requirements of this Indenture.

Model Indenture § 7.01(b)(2).

> The Trustee shall not be liable for any error of judgment made in good faith by a Trust Officer, unless it is proved that the Trustee was negligent in ascertaining the pertinent facts.

Model Indenture § 7.01(c)(2).

> The Trustee may refuse to perform any duty or exercise any right or power which would require it to expend its own funds or risk any liability if it shall reasonably believe that the repayment of such funds or adequate indemnity against such risk is not reasonably assured to it.

Model Indenture § 7.01(c)(4).

The Model Indenture limits the indenture trustee's responsibility to investigate or look behind any document given to it:

> **Section 7.01. Rights of the Trustee**
>
> (a) The Trustee may rely on any document believed by it to be genuine and to have been signed or presented by the proper Person. The Trustee need not investigate any facts or matter stated in the document.
>
> (b) Before the Trustee acts or refrains from acting, it may require an Officer's Certificate or an Opinion of Counsel.

Section 7.01(b) gives the indenture trustee the right to ask the issuer for an officer's certificate and an opinion of counsel before taking any action. This provision is typically invoked when an issuer requests or instructs the indenture trustee to take some action. However, the section is not literally limited to such situations. The indenture trustee's right to request an opinion of counsel has occasionally been invoked where the indenture trustee's rights are unclear, such as a situation where a subsidiary guarantor asserts that it has been automatically released based on an officer's certificate but the legal predicates for the release have been challenged by holders. An indenture trustee may be entitled to an opinion of counsel if one was not provided at the time of the transaction triggering the putative release.

3.8 What is an officer's certificate?

An officer's certificate is a defined term in the indenture. An officer's certificate must include the statements required by the indenture and be signed by an officer specified in the indenture, who must certify that all conditions or covenants relating to a specified event or request of the trustee have been complied with.

> **PRACTICE TIP**
>
> When an indenture refers to an "officers' certificate" as opposed to an "officer's certificate," the signature of more than one officer is required.

3.9 What is an opinion of counsel?

An opinion of counsel, as defined in an indenture, refers to a written opinion of legal counsel stating, among other things, that all conditions or covenants relating to an action or proposed action under the indenture have been met. Indentures will generally require that the legal opinion be from counsel acceptable to the indenture trustee.

An opinion of counsel as defined in the indenture is usually furnished by or on behalf of the issuer, and is different from the written advice of counsel, which refers to the written recommendation provided by counsel consulted by the indenture trustee.

> **PRACTICE TIP**
>
> The definition of "Opinion of Counsel" in the indenture should state that the legal counsel delivering the opinion shall be acceptable to the trustee.

3.10 Does consulting with counsel offer any protection to an indenture trustee?

Yes. Aside from its right to request an opinion of counsel from an issuer, an indenture trustee is entitled to retain its own counsel and rely on that counsel's advice:

> ....The Trustee may also consult with counsel on any matter relating to the Indenture or the Securities and the Trustee shall not be liable for any action it takes or omits to take in good faith in reliance on the advice of counsel.

Model Indenture § 7.02(b).

3.11 Does advice of counsel need to be in writing in order for the indenture trustee to be insulated from liability?

Some indentures state that the advice of counsel must be written. Depending on the context, the writing may be short and informal (such as an email confirming the advice) or it may be long and detailed (such as a "white paper" type memorandum). Decisions as to the form and content of the advice (and as to when written advice will be requested) are made by the indenture trustee, often on a case-by-case basis after consultation with counsel.

PRACTICE TIP

An indenture should not limit the trustee's right to rely on advice of counsel to advice that is "written" or to an "opinion of counsel." Eliminating such limitations will broaden the protection afforded to the indenture trustee.

3.12 Does the advice of counsel need to be reasonable in order for the indenture trustee to rely on it, or for the protection under the indenture to apply?

This issue has not been definitively addressed by the courts. The language of most indentures suggests that the indenture trustee has absolute immunity for following the advice of counsel and is not required to examine or evaluate the accuracy of the legal opinion.

3.13 Can the indenture trustee rely on the written advice of a financial advisor where it has retained a financial advisor in connection with a default?

Yes, but the advice of a financial advisor does not invoke the literal protection of section 7.01(b) of the Model Indenture unless it is relied on and incorporated in the advice of counsel.

3.14 Does the fact that the indenture trustee was directed to take a certain action afford any protection from suits by non-directing holders?

Yes. The Model Indenture provision includes an exculpation provision with respect to following a direction:

> The Trustee shall not be liable with respect to any action it takes or omits to take in good faith in accordance with a direction received by it pursuant to section 6.05.

Model Indenture § 7.01(c)(3).

3.15 When the indenture provides that the trustee shall not be liable, who is bound by this exculpation?

The parties to the indenture are bound by its provisions (*i.e.,* the issuer, any guarantors, and the trustee). Non-parties do not have any contractual rights under the indenture. Strictly speaking, record holders and beneficial holders are not direct parties under the indenture, but they are customarily treated as parties for some purposes, such as direction and consent.

The predominant view is that record holders, as third-party beneficiaries of the indenture, are bound by all provisions of the indenture, including exculpations of the trustee. Beneficial holders are neither direct parties to the indenture nor third-party beneficiaries, but they do enjoy certain rights under the indenture, including the right to direct the trustee. Therefore beneficial holders should arguably be bound by the indenture provisions limiting the liability of the trustee.

3.16 What remedies are typically found in indentures?

Most indentures provide that a trustee may pursue any available remedy to collect the payment of principal and interest due under the indenture, or to enforce the terms of the securities or the indenture. Indentures also provide specific remedies, including acceleration and the filing of a proof of claim in a bankruptcy case. Some indentures provide that acceleration occurs automatically upon the filing of a bankruptcy case, without any action required by the trustee or the holders.

3.17 What is acceleration?

Acceleration means the immediate triggering of all obligations under the indenture, including the payment of all outstanding principal and interest. In other words, acceleration is the immediate occurrence of maturity. An indenture may provide for automatic acceleration upon an event of default, or it may provide that acceleration is a remedy that can be invoked by the indenture trustee (or a requisite percentage of holders in accordance with the applicable provisions of the indenture) upon an event of default.

Acceleration may have implications with respect to the entitlement of holders to a make-whole premium; specifically, acceleration may eliminate the entitlement to a make-whole premium.

Chapter 4. Holders and Directions by Holders

4.1 What is a holder?

The term "holder" is loosely used to mean an investor in a debt security. The term "holder" as defined in the Model Indenture means a person in whose name a debt security is registered.

For purposes of giving consent or direction to the indenture trustee, however, the term, in practice, custom and usage, means beneficial holder (as opposed to registered holder).

The Model Indenture suggests the following language, which reflects the customary usage of the term:

> **Section 6.11 Actions of a Holder.**
>
> For the purpose of providing any consent, waiver or instruction to the Company or the Trustee, a "Holder" or "Securityholder" shall include a Person who provides to the Company or the Trustee, as the case may be, an affidavit of beneficial ownership of a Security together with a satisfactory indemnity against any loss, liability or expense to such party to the extent that it acts upon such affidavit of beneficial ownership (including any consent, waiver or instructions given by a Person providing such affidavit and indemnity).

Model Indenture § 6.11.

4.2 Who are holders?

Holders may be institutional holders, or they may be so-called "retail" holders. Institutional holders are financial institutions, investment banks, insurance companies, managed funds and hedge funds which buy debt securities for their own accounts or for clients. Retail holders are members of the public who are not in the investment business. Retail holders (sometimes called "moms and pops") are typically individuals who purchase debt securities for personal reasons, such as wealth management or income generation.

4.3 What is a "holder in street name"?

A "holder in street name" is the institution (*e.g.*, a broker or custodian) in whose name the securities are held according to the records at DTC. The holder in street name is to be distinguished from the beneficial holder.

4.4 What is a beneficial holder?

A beneficial holder is the true owner of the debt security — the person who has the economic risks and benefits of ownership regardless of who holds the title.

4.5 What is a direction by holders?

Most indentures contain a provision governing control by a majority of holders and the rights of the majority holders to issue directions to the trustee.

For example, the Model Indenture provides:

> **Section 6.05. Control by Majority.**
>
> The Holders of a majority in Principal amount of the Securities may direct the time, method and place of conducting any proceeding for any remedy available to the Trustee or exercising any trust or power conferred on the Trustee. However, the Trustee may refuse to follow any direction that conflicts with law or this Indenture, is unduly prejudicial to the rights of other Securityholders, or would involve the Trustee in

> personal liability or expense for which the Trustee has not received a satisfactory indemnity.

Model Indenture § 6.05.

4.6 Who is a holder for purposes of direction?

Customarily, beneficial holders may direct the indenture trustee, provided they furnish proof of their ownership of the securities as required by the indenture trustee. Some indentures expressly provide that beneficial holders are considered holders for purpose of a direction, *see,* Model Indenture § 6.11, although most indentures do not provide this explicitly.

4.7 When may holders direct the indenture trustee?

Under the terms of a typical indenture, the right of holders to direct the trustee is triggered after an event of default.

4.8 What is the scope of actions that majority holders can direct the indenture trustee to take?

The scope depends on the specific language of the indenture but is generally very broad. Under most indentures, the majority holders can direct any remedial action or the exercise of any right or power conferred on the trustee under the indenture. In practice this is construed broadly, encompassing any aspect of the exercise of any remedy or power available to the indenture trustee. This can include the filing of litigation or taking any action in a bankruptcy case.

A direction can encompass litigation-related decisions, such as where and when to file an action, the form and content of pleadings, and strategic measures as to discovery, motion practice or other litigation case development.

4.9 What is the scope of indemnification that the indenture trustee may require from directing holders?

The scope is determined by the language of the indenture. The Model Indenture, for example, provides that the indenture trustee is entitled to a "satisfactory indemnity," Model Indenture § 6.05.

PRACTICE TIP

Some indentures provide that the indemnity must be satisfactory to the indenture trustee. This language is clearly favorable to the trustee, since the threshold the proposed indemnification needs to meet is not "reasonableness" (leaving open the question as to what is reasonable) but "satisfactory to the trustee." Language providing that the indemnity be "reasonably satisfactory to the trustee" is less favorable to the indenture trustee.

The Model Indenture language which provides that the indenture trustee is entitled to a "satisfactory indemnity" prescribes an objective standard, as contrasted with the more trustee-centric "satisfactory to the trustee." The alternative language — "reasonably satisfactory to the indenture trustee" — makes it clear that the determination is to be made by the indenture trustee, but that the trustee's determination must be reasonable.

In practice, all three formulations are found in indentures.

4.10 What type of indemnification may the indenture trustee require in order to follow a direction?

The nature of the indemnification is determined by the indenture trustee on a case by case basis, depending on the nature of the direction. Some directions are discrete: for example, a direction to retain an appraiser for a flat fee. Other directions are more open ended insofar as costs are concerned: for example, a direction to file a lawsuit against the issuer.

Some directions may carry a potential for liability beyond merely the direct costs that result from following the direction. For example, an indenture trustee's filing an involuntary petition may lead the debtor to seek sanctions against the trustee as a petitioning creditor under Bankruptcy Code § 303(i).

Some typical indemnification requirements include:

- An agreement to pay invoices of professionals retained and other expenses incurred by the indenture trustee in connection with complying with the direction
- Demonstration of liquid assets available to satisfy the indemnification
- Payment of an advance to cover expenses that will be incurred in complying with the direction
- Signatures of affiliates or other guarantors, if the directing holder has insufficient resources to provide a sufficient guarantee of payment to the indenture trustee

4.11 Can holders direct the indenture trustee to retain a specific law firm or financial advisor, and must the indenture trustee follow such a direction?

Holders may wish to direct the indenture trustee to engage a particular firm or financial advisor. As with any direction, such direction will be subject to the qualifications described in the indenture (such as the second sentence of section 6.05 of the Model Indenture). The indenture trustee may refuse to follow the direction if it prejudices other holders or would expose the trustee to liability for which it has not been satisfactorily indemnified.

Provided that the indenture trustee has determined that following the direction would not prejudice other holders or expose it to liability for which it has not been indemnified, the indenture trustee will often follow the direction but impose conditions. These conditions may include both financial and non-financial agreements on the part of the directing holders, as part of the indemnification required by the indenture trustee. Financial conditions include the payment and guarantee arrangements that the indenture trustee will require to cover the costs and any potential liability that may arise as a result of following the direction.

The indenture trustee may also impose non-financial conditions as well. One such typical condition is that the indenture trustee may retain independent counsel (often to serve as co-counsel with the law firm the indenture trustee is being directed to hire) and that the fees of the indenture trustee and independent counsel will be paid by the directing holders. The reason for this condition is to ensure that any action taken represents the interests of the indenture trustee and the non-directing holders as well as the interests of the directing holders.

4.12 Can holders direct the indenture trustee to treat expenses incurred by the directing holders as expenses of the trustee under the indenture?

This is a controversial question. This type of direction sometimes arises where the directing holder or group of holders have been working with a law firm or advisor for some time, and costs have been incurred which the holders wish to be paid by the indenture trustee out of the eventual recovery, as opposed to being borne or advanced by the directing holders. In this scenario, the directing holders seek to have the indenture trustee treat the expense as an expense of the indenture trustee, to be paid through the exercise of the indenture trustee's charging lien, as a first priority expense. *See* Model Indenture § 6.08. In most instances, the holders will also direct the indenture trustee to retain the firm that has been representing a group of holders and to assume the fees and expenses incurred during the time period in which the firm was representing only the directing holders.

This question may also arise where a group of holders has undertaken a strategy involving the infusion of new money (such as a debtor-in-possession credit facility or exit financing through a rights offering) and incurs fees and expenses in connection with the transaction. This strategy may benefit all holders collectively because it may strengthen the negotiating position of the holders engaged in the new money transaction, which in turn may improve the recovery for all holders.

This type of direction is not the norm and generally is disfavored. The decision whether to follow such a direction is made on a case-by-case basis by each indenture trustee, based on the particular circumstances as well as the indenture trustee's internal corporate trust policies. In some cases, an indenture trustee may decide to follow such direction if the indenture trustee views the work done by the firm for a holder or group of holders prior to its retention by the indenture trustee to be beneficial to all the holders collectively. The indenture trustee will generally require that the firm provide the indenture trustee with its entire work product produced during the time period for which the payment is sought.

Where the work created no discernible benefit to the holders collectively or the indenture trustee, the direction is not appropriate. In particular, work done for individual holders in connection with the purchase or sale of their securities is not an appropriate expense of the indenture trustee. Similarly, work done in connection with an equity or other investment which uniquely benefits only certain holders is rarely, if ever, considered a trustee expense. On the other hand, preparing litigation to be filed by the indenture trustee to enforce the obligations under the indenture or in connection with the securities may be deemed appropriate by the indenture trustee. The decision whether to treat such expenses as trustee expenses rests solely in the indenture trustee's discretion.

Chapter 5. The Depository Trust Company

5.1 What is DTC?

DTC is The Depository Trust Company, a subsidiary of Depository Trust & Clearing Corporation (DTCC). DTCC is owned by the largest banks, brokers, and dealers in securities, which are the DTC participants.

DTC was created in 1973 to provide services to the securities industry. DTC performs three types of functions: a depository for safekeeping of securities, an electronic record-keeper, and a clearing house for settlement. DTC's three main functions — that of custodian, record-keeper, and clearing house — are seamlessly interconnected. As paper securities became increasingly rare, electronic record keeping and clearing became more essential.

In Europe, there are two large securities depositories, Euroclear and Clearstream, which perform functions similar to DTC.

5.2 Why are DTC's services as a depository and electronic record-keeper necessary?

While some securities are certificated (held by individual holders in the form of a paper certificate), most securities can be, and are, held in book entry form. Having a centralized depository, record-keeper, and clearing house creates speed, accuracy, and efficiency, and is necessary to facilitate securities transactions. DTC has custody of trillions of dollars of securities in the United States and abroad.

Bonds held in book entry form are held in the name of a nominee or common depository for the relevant clearing system (*e.g.*, DTC,

Euroclear, or Clearstream). DTC's nominee is Cede & Co. Securities held in book entry form through DTC are in the name of Cede & Co.

Euroclear and Clearstream hold positions in securities within a common depository which is typically a bank entity related to the indenture trustee. Securities held through Euroclear or Clearstream are registered in the name of the nominee of the common depositary.

5.3 What is a global note?

A global note is a certificate representing the outstanding securities of a class or series which is deposited with DTC or its custodian. DTC's nominee Cede and Co. holds the global securities on behalf of all the DTC participants and is the registered holder of the securities.

DTC electronically processes interest payments and facilitates trades of interests in securities among participants. Through its systems, DTC acts as a record keeper for the sale and purchase of securities among DTC participants for the benefit of their customers, which include beneficial holders of the securities.

A chapter 11 plan will sometimes provide for cash distributions and/or issuance of new securities to the beneficial holders of debt securities. Upon instruction, DTC handles the allocation and distribution of cash and/or new securities to the appropriate participant (often an investment bank or broker/dealer), which in turn transmits such distributions to its customers.

5.4 What is a CUSIP?

Securities held at DTC are identified by alpha-numeric codes called CUSIPs. CUSIP is the acronym for "Committee on Uniform Security Identification Procedures," a committee of the American Bankers Association which developed the CUSIP system. CUSIPs are obtained by the issuer. The indenture trustee does not issue or assign CUSIPs, nor does it ensure the eligibility of such CUSIP'S within DTC.

5.5 What is an ISIN?

Securities held at Euroclear and Clearstream are identified by codes similar to CUSIPs, known as ISINs. ISIN stands for "International Securities Identification Number."

5.6 Does DTC maintain lists of beneficial holders?

No. DTC can provide the indenture trustee with a security position report (SPR) but this report only indicates the DTC's participants' positions with respect to the security.

5.7 Does the indenture trustee maintain records of the holders of a security?

No, not as a matter of course. The indenture trustee can obtain the SPR from DTC but as noted above this report only indicates the DTC participants' positions with respect to the security.

It is often difficult to identify beneficial holders. Identities of beneficial holders are not readily obtainable by either an indenture trustee or an issuer. DTC participants are responsible for distributing notices and ballots to their customers (*e.g.*, beneficial owners).

There are a number of vendors who provide services to identify and locate the beneficial holders and their holdings. This is often needed in a chapter 11 case in order for a debtor to have direct communications with beneficial holders, particularly during the plan process, including negotiating and, ultimately, soliciting votes for a plan.

5.8 What is DTC's function in the bankruptcy case of an issuer?

DTC performs a number of important functions. DTC handles posting of notices from the indenture trustee and transmits them to its participants.

DTC also handles the transmission of cash and securities distributed to holders during a bankruptcy, most commonly under a confirmed chapter 11 plan.

Participants are responsible for redistribution of notices, cash, and securities distributions to their customers for ultimate delivery to beneficial holders.

5.9 What is LENS?

DTC's Legal Notice System (LENS) is an online data base of notices regarding DTC-eligible securities. LENS allows participants and other users to access and search for notices by CUSIP, keyword, notice type or LENS document number. Users can also register for email alerts.

5.10 What are DTC's procedures on effectuating distributions to holders under a chapter 11 plan?

DTC's procedures are extensive, and change from time to time. The following is a summary of DTC's basic procedures that often come into play in a bankruptcy distribution.

DTC transmits payments or securities to participants for distribution to the ultimate beneficial holders. When distributions are made by a debtor issuer (for example, under a chapter 11 plan) to the indenture trustee, as paying agent, the indenture trustee/paying agent in turn wires the funds or allocates the securities with instructions to DTC. DTC in turn distributes the funds or securities to participants in accordance with those instructions.

PART II

THE INDENTURE TRUSTEE

PART II:

The Indenture Trustee

Chapter 6. Compensation and Indemnity

6.1 Does an indenture trustee have the right to be compensated and indemnified in connection with its role under an indenture?

Yes. Every indenture provides for compensation and indemnification of the indenture trustee. As a business matter, no institution would provide a service for which it is not to be paid. Further, because acting as indenture trustee involves extensive work in a default situation and carries with it the risk that a defaulting issuer may be unwilling or unable to pay, no corporate trust provider would accept indenture trustee appointments without indenture mechanisms that enhance its rights to payment in a default situation.

Indentures typically provide both for compensation and indemnification by the issuer, as well as a priority of payment and charging lien rights, in the event of default.

An example of such provisions is found in the Model Indenture:

> **Section 7.07. Compensation and Indemnity**
>
> The Company shall pay to the Trustee from time to time reasonable compensation for its services, including for any Agent capacity in which it acts. The Trustee's compensation shall not be limited by any law

on compensation of a trustee of an express trust. The Company shall reimburse the Trustee upon request for all reasonable out-of-pocket expenses incurred by it. Such expenses shall include the reasonable compensation and out-of-pocket expenses of the Trustee's agents and counsel.

The Company shall indemnify the Trustee against any loss, liability or expense incurred by it including in any Agent capacity in which it acts. The Trustee shall notify the Company promptly of any claim for which it may seek indemnity. The Company shall defend the claim and the Trustee shall cooperate in the defense. The Trustee may have separate counsel and the Company shall pay the reasonable fees and expenses of such counsel. The Company need not pay for any settlement made without its consent, which consent shall not unreasonably be withheld.

The Company need not reimburse any expense or indemnify against any loss or liability incurred by the Trustee through gross negligence, willful misconduct or bad faith.

To secure the Company's payment obligations in this Section, the Trustee shall have a lien prior to the Securities on all money or property held or collected by the Trustee, except that held in trust to pay Principal and interest on particular Securities.

Without prejudice to its rights hereunder, when the Trustee incurs expenses or renders services

> after [a bankruptcy filing] occurs, the expenses and the compensation for the services are intended to constitute expenses of administration under any Bankruptcy Law.

Model Indenture § 7.07.

PRACTICE TIP

Some indentures improve upon the Model Indenture language by specifying that the indemnity is intended to cover (1) any predecessor trustee; (2) the trustee's officers, agents, directors and employees; (3) all claims arising or in connection with the indenture or the securities, whether brought by the issuer, a holder, or any other person; and (4) defense costs, including fees and expenses of counsel and taxes (other than taxes based upon, measured by, or determined by the income of the trustee).

6.2 What types of fees and expenses are typically charged by an indenture trustee in a default scenario?

In addition to its standard annual fees for the administration of the indenture, trustees charge hourly fees for their default administration services. These are referred to as "extraordinary fees" because they are not ordinary or administrative, but are incurred only when an extraordinary event occurs, such as the default of the issuer.

During a bankruptcy case, the indenture trustee continues to charge annual administration fees. Indenture trustees also charge a fee for each distribution handled in a bankruptcy case. These fees vary by institution and often by the size, nature, and complexity of the distribution involved.

The indenture trustee is also entitled to reimbursement of expenses, including the fees and expenses of professionals. Indentures generally provide that after an event of default, the indenture trustee may retain legal counsel of its choosing. While most indentures do not specifically mention the retention of any professional except counsel, the indenture trustee is permitted to engage agents, which may include financial advisors or other consultants or professionals as necessary. In a bankruptcy or default situation, the services of an appraiser, expert witness or other consultant may be necessary or appropriate to enforce remedies under the indenture.

PRACTICE TIP

The indenture trustee's post-default services, including serving on an *ad hoc* holder committee or an official committee (a "Committee") in a chapter 11 case, constitute extraordinary services for which premium rate hourly fees are typically charged.

Indenture trustees are also entitled to annual fees under the indenture, as well as distribution fees in connection with handling interim and final distributions in a bankruptcy case.

6.3 What is the default waterfall?

The default waterfall refers to the provisions for priority of payments after an event of default. Such provisions state that after an event of default, all money or other property distributable in respect of the issuer's obligations under the indenture shall be applied by the indenture trustee as follows: *first,* to amounts due it under the compensation and indemnification provisions of the indenture, and, *second*, to holders for principal and interest due and outstanding. *See* Model Indenture § 6.08.

PRACTICE TIP

To avoid the risk that the waterfall does not encompass all funds or property potentially available, the indenture language should be broad. Preferred language is:

> Any money collected by the Trustee pursuant to this Article, or, after an Event of Default, any money or other property distributable or allocable in respect of the Company's obligations under this Indenture shall be applied in the following order:
>
> First: To the payment of all amounts payable to the Trustee (including any predecessor trustee)[.]

6.4 What is an indenture trustee's charging lien?

The indenture trustee's charging lien is a contractual, possessory lien of the indenture trustee, which is provided for in an indenture. The charging lien secures the payment of the fees, expenses, and indemnification claims of the indenture trustee.

For example, the Model Indenture provides for a charging lien as follows:

> To secure the Company's payment obligations in this Section, the Trustee shall have a lien prior to the Securities on all money or property held or collected by the Trustee, except that held in trust to pay Principal and interest on particular Securities.

Model Indenture § 7.07.

The default waterfall, which provides that the indenture trustee may first apply any funds coming into its hands after an event of default to pay its fees and expenses, is the functional equivalent of a charging lien. Most indentures also contain an explicit grant of a charging lien to the indenture trustee.

6.5 What is the relationship between the charging lien and the priority of payment provisions?

The charging lien and priority payment provisions should be consistent and coextensive. Under the priority of payment provisions of the indenture (sometimes referred to as the "default waterfall" provisions), the amounts owed to the trustee for its fees, expenses and indemnification rights — amounts for which the indenture trustee has a charging lien — may be deducted from funds coming into the indenture trustee's hands before funds are distributed to holders. The charging lien provides the indenture trustee with a contractual, possessory lien in those amounts.

In a properly drafted indenture, both the default waterfall provision and the charging lien provision will refer to the compensation and indemnity section of the indenture. The charging lien grant is often actually contained in the compensation and indemnification section as suggested by the Model Indenture. While arguably redundant, modern indentures expressly provide for both a charging lien and priority of payment.

6.6 Why do indentures have charging lien and priority of payment provisions?

Such provisions are critically important to the corporate trustee's business model. The reason for the payment priority and/or charging lien is to provide a method for the indenture trustee to be reimbursed for work performed on behalf of the holders. Absent such provisions in indentures, there would be no business case for banks and other institutional trustees to provide corporate trust services. It would not make business sense for an institution to take on an indenture trustee role when it would not be paid its fees and expenses in a default situation.

6.7 What type of expenses can be paid by an indenture trustee through the exercise of its charging lien or under the default waterfall provisions?

Any fees and expenses which the indenture trustee incurs in connection with the administration of the indenture, and/or the exercise of its rights, powers or duties under the indenture following an event of default may be paid under the default waterfall provision. This includes fees for the trustee's work done in connection with the default of the issuer, as well as expenses, which include the fees and expenses of the indenture trustee's counsel and advisors. The basis for the trustee's entitlement in the first instance is the compensation and indemnification provisions of the indenture, such as those found in section 7.07 of the Model Indenture.

6.8 What liabilities are covered by the trustee's indemnity under the indenture?

The scope of the indemnification will be determined by the language of the Indenture. The Model Indenture language ("The Company shall indemnify the Trustee against any loss, liability or expense") is intended to encompass attorneys' fees and costs, as well as losses or damages imposed in litigation. Model Indenture § 7.07.

Under TIA § 315(d), a TIA-qualified indenture may not relieve the trustee from liability for its own negligent action, negligent failure to act or willful misconduct, subject to the exceptions set forth in TIA § 315(d)(1)-(3). Similar language is also found in non-TIA indentures.

PRACTICE TIP

Under New York law, which governs most indentures, indemnities are strictly construed. In order for an indemnification to cover attorneys' fees, the indemnification provision must unequivocally cover disputes between the contracting parties. *Hooper Assocs. v. AGS Computers,* 74 N.Y.2d 487, 491, 549 N.Y.S.2d 365, 366-67 (1989).

An example of unequivocal language in an indenture is:

> The Issuer and the Guarantors, jointly and severally, shall indemnify the Trustee and any predecessor trustee and their officers, agents, directors, and employees for any and all loss, damage, claims, liability or expense (including attorneys fees) incurred by the Trustee in connection with the Indenture, and the performance of its duties hereunder, or with the securities, including, without limitation, the costs of enforcing this Indenture against the Issuer or any of the Guarantors, including rights under this section, or defending itself against any claim brought by the Issuer, a Guarantor, any Holder or holder, or any other person, or any liability in connection with the acceptance, exercise or performance of any of its powers or duties hereunder, or in connection with enforcing the provisions of this section.

6.9 May the indenture trustee exercise its charging lien to reserve funds necessary to cover future anticipated expenses?

As a matter of industry practice, indenture trustees exercise their charging lien to create a reserve for future anticipated expenses. While there is a dearth of case law on this question, the prevailing view is that the reserve must be reasonable. *See Bluebird Partners, L.P. v. Bank of New York*, Index No.: 601016/96, 2010 N.Y. Misc. LEXIS 2503, at *10–11 (Sup. Ct. N.Y. Cnty. June 7, 2010).

While a standard indenture does not state specifically that the trustee may establish a reserve for fees and expenses, the typical language can be read to provide such a right. The indenture trustee's charging lien secures its indemnity claims. Because the indenture trustee has a present indemnity claim for future expenses, the charging lien can encompass fees and expenses that the trustee reasonably expects to be incurred.

PRACTICE TIP

The *Bluebird* case suggests that, in establishing a reserve for fees and expenses, including litigation expenses, the indenture trustee must act as a prudent person in determining the amount of reserves.

Prudent measures which an indenture trustee may take in determining the amount of a reserve include:

- Soliciting estimates of projected fees and expenses from professionals
- Analyzing estimated fees and expenses, and increasing them by a reasonable cushion (such as 10%)
- Consulting the corporate trust or default advisory committee
- Obtaining advice of counsel regarding the reasonableness of the reserve

Chapter 7. Retention of Professionals

7.1 Does the indenture trustee have the right to retain counsel?

Yes. Indentures expressly provide that the trustee may also consult with counsel on any matter relating to the indenture. *See* Model Indenture § 7.02(b). Indentures also provide that the indenture trustee is entitled to be reimbursed by the issuer for reasonable out of pocket expenses, including the expense of the trustee's agents and counsel. *See* Model Indenture § 7.07.

7.2 Does the indenture trustee have the right to retain financial advisors and consultants?

Yes. Most indentures do not expressly refer to financial advisors or consultants. However, the indenture language allowing for retention or payment of agents is construed in industry practice to allow the retention of financial advisors, appraisers, or other consultants as may be necessary in the exercise of rights and performance of duties in a default situation.

7.3 When should the indenture trustee retain counsel or other professionals?

Following an event of default, the indenture trustee should have counsel. Under most court rules, only individuals may appear without counsel. An indenture trustee, as a corporate entity, is not allowed to appear or represent itself in court, except by counsel. Thus, without counsel, an indenture trustee could not initiate an action against the issuer, nor could the indenture trustee appear in a legal proceeding, such as a bankruptcy case. As the exercise of remedies often requires a legal proceeding, and an event of default is frequently followed by a bankruptcy filing, counsel is inevitably required after an event of default.

Moreover, if the issuer has filed or is expected to file a bankruptcy, under the prudent person standard, an indenture trustee should retain a lawyer with core competence in the area of bankruptcy. Bankruptcy is a complex legal proceeding in which an expert, experienced bankruptcy lawyer is necessary.

An indenture trustee may also need to retain consulting experts and expert witnesses in litigation. Indenture trustees should obtain their counsel's written recommendation advising the retention.

Another professional sometimes retained by an indenture trustee is an appraiser. An appraiser is retained when the indenture trustee needs a valuation of collateral to evaluate remedies or recovery options, such as a foreclosure.

7.4 Does an indenture trustee require a direction in order to retain professionals?

No. However, an indenture trustee will generally require a written direction and indemnification before retaining professionals selected by holders for a specific purpose, such as commencing an action. The retention would normally be part of the direction by the holders to file the action.

7.5 How does an indenture trustee retain professionals given that it is not obligated under the indenture to expend its own funds?

Generally speaking, the indenture trustee is not required to take any action which would require it to expand its own funds or risk any liability. *See, e.g.*, Model Indenture § 7.01(c)(4). However, the duty to act as a prudent person following an event of default often means the retention of counsel, particularly in a bankruptcy proceeding. In the corporate trust industry, trustees generally require counsel to undertake the representation on a non-recourse basis, *i.e.*, the firm to be retained must agree to look solely to the issuer (or to the proceeds of recovery) for payment, and not to the indenture trustee.

When an indenture trustee is directed by holders to retain a law firm or other professional, the indenture trustee will require that either (1) the fees and costs of the firm to be retained be advanced by the directing holders, or (2) the firm agree to be paid on a non-recourse basis, with the fees and expenses to be paid entirely from a recovery and without any obligation on the part of the indenture trustee.

PRACTICE TIP

Indenture trustees often require non-recourse language in any engagement letter with any professional, including law firms or financial advisors. An example of such language is as follows:

> In matters involving default and bankruptcy services, the obligation of ABC Corporate Trust Company ("ABC") for fees and expenses will be limited to: (1) amounts recovered by ABC from the issuer/obligor for whom ABC serves as indenture trustee; (2) any recoveries on behalf of the holders of the securities for whom ABC serves as indenture trustee; (3) the security holders themselves, to the extent such holders advance such fees and expenses; or (4) any other sources of payment or reimbursement to ABC on account of the securities (collectively, the "Trust Sources"). The Firm agrees that ABC is not individually liable for the Firm's fees and expenses, and will have no liability or obligation to pay such fees and expenses, except as set forth above.

> In the event that amounts recovered from Trust Sources are insufficient to pay in full the claims of both ABC and the Firm, the amounts recovered will be applied *pro rata* between ABC and the Firm in proportion to the total fees and expenses incurred.

7.6 May an indenture trustee indemnify a professional which requires indemnification in the professional's retention agreement?

This question is most often presented in connection with the retention of financial advisory firms which require indemnification as part of their engagement. Most corporate trust providers have a policy of not indemnifying vendors or agents, including financial advisors. This frequently presents a dilemma, when an indenture trustee seeks to retain (or is directed to retain) a financial advisor which requires indemnification as part of its standard retention agreement.

Indentures do not expressly authorize the indenture trustee to provide indemnification. Some indentures provide that the issuer shall indemnify the trustee and its agents. This language would provide the indenture trustee with a basis to confirm, in its engagement letter with a financial advisor, that the financial advisor is an agent for purposes of the indemnification contained in the indenture.

Ideally, the issuer would acknowledge that the indemnification in the indenture covers the indenture trustee's proposed financial advisor. The issuer may be unwilling to provide such acknowledgement, particularly following an event of default, where the relationship between the indenture trustee and the issuer is adverse.

7.7 May a trustee obtain an advance or loan to pay fees and expenses incurred in the exercise of remedies under the indenture?

Incurring a loan to pay fees and expenses is neither expressly authorized nor expressly prohibited under most indentures. While rare, such loans are not unprecedented, and are sometimes made by holders of the debt securities to facilitate or enable a retention of counsel and/or financial advisors.

The cost of a loan to pay expenses of professionals expends itself against the recovery of all holders. This is controversial because a loan may be unnecessary: many professionals will represent indenture trustees on a non-recourse basis and do not require the current payment of fees in order to provide representation.

In incurring such a loan, an indenture trustee will ordinarily, at a minimum, require the following:

- The loan must be non-recourse to the trustee and must be payable only from funds collected by the trustee under the indenture. The trustee must not be obligated under the loan in its individual capacity.
- The arrangement must be in the interest of all holders.
- Notice of the proposed arrangement must be provided to all holders with a reasonable opportunity to object.
- The costs of the loan (interest and fees, including reimbursement of legal expenses and a lending fee) must be reasonable.
- The trustee will normally require direction and indemnification by holders owning a majority in principal amount of the outstanding securities.

Whether a trustee will enter into a loan agreement to finance costs is a matter within the trustee's sole discretion in light of its internal corporate trust policies.

Chapter 8. Conflicts and Replacement of the Indenture Trustee

8.1 What standards govern an indenture trustee's obligation to avoid conflicts of interest?

An indenture trustee is required to avoid conflicts of interest. With respect to indentures governed by the Trust Indenture Act, conflicting interests are defined and enumerated in the TIA. Similar provisions are also found in non-TIA qualified indentures. A number of courts have also addressed the obligation of the indenture trustee to avoid conflicts of interest as a matter of common law, whether or not an indenture is governed by the TIA.

Section 310 of the TIA explicitly defines situations that present conflicting interests if the securities are in default and require the resignation of a trustee and the appointment of a successor.

8.2 What is a typical instance of a conflict requiring resignation under the TIA?

The most common conflict occurs when the same institution is the trustee under more than one indenture. TIA § 310(b)(1). For example, if the same institution is the indenture trustee under both a first lien indenture and a second lien indenture, under both a secured indenture and an unsecured indenture, or under both senior and subordinated indentures, conflicting interests are presented which require resignation.

The trustee may remain as trustee under more than one indenture if both indentures are wholly unsecured and rank equally. Trustees, however, sometimes choose to resign even in that situation, particularly if there are differences in the guarantors of the two indentures or in other material terms. An indenture trustee may decide to do so to avoid an appearance of a conflict in the event the trustee needs to advocate for additional rights on behalf of one set of holders, which rights do not apply to the holders under the other indenture. While this is neither a statutory nor other conflict, the indenture trustee may decide to resign at its discretion.

Another common situation is where the indenture trustee is also a creditor of the issuer (for example, a lender under a commercial loan facility), creating a conflicting interest upon default and requiring resignation under TIA § 310(b)(10).

8.3 If the indenture trustee does not have a conflict under the TIA, can a conflict nonetheless exist?

TIA § 310 (b) was not written as a safe harbor. The universe of conflicts of interests with respect to a TIA-governed indenture may not be limited to those defined in the TIA. A few courts have held that the obligation to avoid conflicts of interest is not confined to conflicts defined by the TIA, but is a duty under common law. *See United States Trust Co. of N.Y. v. First Nat'l City Bank*, 57 A.D. 2d 285, 295-97, 394 N.Y.S.2d 653, 660-61 (1st Dept. 1977), *aff'd,* 45 N.Y.2d 869, 410 N.Y.S.2d 580 (1978); *In re E.F. Hutton Southwest Properties II, Ltd.* 953 F.2d. 963, 969-72 (5th Cir. 1992). Therefore, indenture trustees should look not only at the TIA where applicable, but also to state law to assess potential conflicts of interest.

8.4 Which state's law applies to an indenture trustee with respect to conflicts of interest?

The choice of law provisions in the indenture generally apply. The vast majority of TIA-governed indentures provide that they are governed by New York law. Many non-TIA indentures are governed by New York law as well. Not surprisingly, there are several reported cases in New York addressing conflicts of interest.

While not specifically stated in indentures, avoiding conflicts of interest and discharging its obligations with singleness of purpose and loyalty are duties which New York courts have imposed upon indenture trustees. Courts have likened the duty of an indenture trustee after an issuer's default to that of a fiduciary. *Beck v. Manufacturers Hanover Trust Co.*, 218 A.D.2d 1, 10-12, 632 N.Y.S.2d 520, 526-27 (1st Dep't 1995).

8.5 What circumstances give rise to a conflict under state or common law?

The courts have usually addressed alleged conflicts (either present or potential) where a holder has asserted that it incurred a loss based on a trustee's alleged conflict of interest. Where an indenture trustee is also a lender, and takes action as a lender which directly injures the bondholders for which it is a trustee, a conflict of interest is present. *Dabney v. Chase Nat'l Bank of City of N.Y.*, 196 F.2d 668, 675 (2d Cir. 1952), *opinion supplemented by*, 201 F.2d 635 (2d Cir. 1953). In *Dabney*, the indenture trustee proceeded to collect a loan in the face of an obligor's insolvency. The court considered the indenture trustee as foreseeably disadvantaging its debenture holders while providing itself as lender with a financial advantage.

If the same circumstances had occurred under a TIA-governed indenture — in other words, if the indenture trustee were a creditor (for example, under a loan facility with the issuer) and an event of default under the indenture occurred — the indenture trustee would be required to resign under TIA § 310. *Dabney* suggests that, in situations where the indenture trustee is also a creditor of the issuer's in a lending relationship and a default occurs, resignation is required, even if the TIA is inapplicable to the indenture.

Conversely, at least one New York court has held that where the indenture trustee has no financial interest, it cannot have a conflict of interest, even if it has multiple roles. *Hildene Capital Mgmt., LLC v. The Bank of New York Mellon,* Index No. 650980/10, J. O. Peter Sherwood, at *10 (Sup. Ct. N.Y. Cnty. Jan. 5, 2015).

8.6 What is an indenture trustee required to do when a conflict is present?

Under the TIA, the indenture trustee, within 90 days of ascertaining that it has a conflict, must either eliminate the conflict or resign (in which case the issuer must take prompt steps to have a successor appointed). TIA § 310(b)(i).[4]

8.7 How is the resignation of an indenture trustee and the appointment of a successor usually accomplished?

The Model Indenture provides that the indenture trustee may resign by notifying the issuer, and the issuer shall appoint a successor trustee. In practice, the resigning trustee usually identifies a successor and requests that the issuer enter into an agreement providing for the resignation of the resigning trustee and the appointment of a successor trustee.[5]

8.8 May holders remove the indenture trustee?

Holders may remove the indenture trustee under the circumstances specified in the indenture. For example, section 7.08 of the Model Indenture provides:

> The Holders of a majority in Principal amount of the Securities may remove the Trustee by so notifying the Trustee and the Company. The Company may remove the Trustee if:
>
> (1) the Trustee fails to comply with Section 7.10;
>
> (2) the Trustee is adjudged a bankrupt or an insolvent;

> (3) a receiver or public officer takes charge of the Trustee or its property; or
>
> (4) the Trustee becomes incapable of acting.
>
> If the Trustee resigns or is removed or if a vacancy exists in the office of Trustee for any reason, the Company shall promptly appoint a successor Trustee.

Model Indenture, section 7.08.

8.9 May holders replace the indenture trustee?

In most indentures, the successor trustee may only be appointed by the issuer, not the holders. Issuers typically rely on the resigning trustee to propose a successor and rarely object to or refuse to accept the recommendation of the resigning trustee as to its successor.

PRACTICE TIP

Considerations for a Successor Trustee

Before accepting a successorship, a potential successor trustee will review and assess the transaction to determine, as a business and legal matter, the potential risks and benefits of the appointment.

Some typical due diligence items include:

Reviewing the Documents

- Does the successor trustee meet the eligibility requirements in the indenture, including the capital requirements?
- Is the language of the indenture standard, including the provisions regarding the rights and duties of the trustee and the standard of care and immunities?
- Does the resigning trustee have a complete set of transactional documents, including collateral documents, if applicable?

Compensation and Indemnification Provisions

- Is the language standard?
- Are the indenture trustee's fees and expenses required to be "reasonable"?
- Do the default waterfall and priority of payment provisions cover all of the indenture trustee's fees, expenses, compensation and indemnification claims?
- Is there a charging lien and what is its scope?
- Are all funds from any source subject to the waterfall and charging lien?
- In a subordinated indenture, are the trustee's fees and expenses subordinated to senior note holders?

Reviewing the Collateral

- What is the collateral?
- Are there reserve accounts and, if so, can the trustee use them for its fees and expenses?
- What sources of payment exist under the indenture?
- Are liens perfected?
- Is the collateral at legal or physical risk?

8.10 If there is no issuer to appoint a successor or enter into an agreement providing for a resignation and successorship, how can a resigning trustee accomplish a transition to a successor?

Where the issuer no longer exists or has the ability to sign an agreement, the resigning trustee can seek a court order appointing a successor.

PART III

POST-DEFAULT ADMINISTRATION

PART III:

Post-Default Administration

Chapter 9. Notices

9.1 What is a notice to holders?

A notice to holders is a written communication from the indenture trustee to all holders of a debt security.

9.2 When does an indenture trustee provide notice to holders?

The Trust Indenture Act (and most indentures, whether or not governed by the TIA) provide that the indenture trustee shall give notice of a default to holders within 90 days of the default. Section 315(b) of the TIA provides:

> (b) Notice of defaults
>
> The indenture trustee shall give to the indenture security holders, in the manner and to the extent provided in subsection (c) of section 313, notice of all defaults known to the trustee, within ninety days after the occurrence thereof: *Provided*, That such indenture shall automatically be deemed (unless it is expressly provided therein that such provision is excluded) to provide that, except in the case of default in the payment of the principal of or interest on any indenture security, or in the payment of any sinking or purchase fund

> installment, the trustee shall be protected in withholding such notice if, and so long as, the board of directors, the executive committee, or a trust committee of directors and/or responsible officers, of the trustee in good faith determine that the withholding of such notice is in the interests of the indenture security holders.

TIA § 315(b).

9.3 Under what circumstances might an indenture trustee determine to withhold notice of a default?

Such instances are rare. Withholding a notice of default is governed by the indenture, and typically occurs where the board, executive committee, trust committee or responsible officers of the indenture trustee determine that withholding of the notice is in the interest of the holders. Such a circumstance might be present, for example, if the anticipated publicity regarding the indenture trustee's notice of default would jeopardize a transaction involving the issuer which was value-enhancing for the holders, or if the notice of default would itself trigger a forfeiture or other consequences to the issuer or its assets which would diminish the recovery value to holders.

9.4 Other than the occurrence of a default, are there other circumstances under which the indenture trustee might provide notice?

Other than the occurrence of a default or a failure to timely resign because of a conflict of interest,[6] indentures generally are not specific as to what events trigger the trustee's obligation to provide notice to holders. In practice, there are a number of other instances in which notices are customarily provided, even though not specifically required by the indenture.

Following a bankruptcy filing (which is itself an event of default under most indentures, triggering a requirement to provide notice), the indenture trustee typically provides notice of material developments in the bankruptcy case which affect holders. In addition, some indenture trustees also provide periodic or annual notices during a bankruptcy case, even in the absence of material developments. Such notices, which are not explicitly required under the indenture, are within the trustee's discretion and are solely a matter of practice and policy of the trustee.

9.5 Why do indenture trustees provide periodic notices to holders of events occurring during a bankruptcy case?

While such notices are not required under the standard indenture, the prevalent practice among indenture trustees is to provide periodic notices of material events affecting holders during a chapter 11 case.

Notices to holders serve several important purposes:

- Notices ensure that uniform information is being provided to all holders at the same time.
- Notices are efficient and obviate many inquiries by holders.
- Notices protect the indenture trustee. Courts have often considered the fact that an indenture trustee provided notice to holders of a proposed action or inaction as a significant factor in determining whether the trustee acted in accordance with its duty as a prudent person.

9.6 What kind of bankruptcy events are contained in indenture trustees' notices to holders?

Events which are the subject of notices include:

- The appointment of a Committee
- The appointment of the indenture trustee to the Committee
- The retention of professionals by the Committee
- The retention of professionals by the indenture trustee
- The URL of any website established with information concerning the chapter 11 case

- The approval of sale procedures for substantially all of the assets of the debtor
- The appointment of an examiner or a bankruptcy trustee
- The establishment of a bar date for filing claims
- The filing of a proof of claim by the indenture trustee
- The filing of a lawsuit or adversary proceeding by or against the indenture trustee
- The filing of a disclosure statement and plan (including relevant deadlines and hearings)
- Plan confirmation and the effective date of the plan
- Distributions to holders (interim and final)

9.7 What are the contents of an indenture trustee's notice to holders?

The contents are usually confined to factual information which is a matter of public record (such as court filings) and which the indenture trustee deems pertinent to the debt securities. Notices should not contain confidential or material non-public information, nor should they provide the indenture trustee's advice or recommendations.

The notice may contain information as to actions the indenture trustee is going to take, and provide an opportunity for holders to comment, object, provide a written direction to the trustee, or seek judicial relief.

PRACTICE TIP

Most indenture trustees include certain disclaimer language in their notices, including disclaimers as to:

- the correctness of CUSIP numbers;
- reliance on the indenture trustee as the sole source of information;

- the fact that the indenture trustee is not providing any legal, investment, tax or other recommendations or advice.

Here are some examples of typical disclaimers:

> The CUSIP numbers are included herein solely for the convenience of the registered holders of the Notes. No representation is made as to the correctness or accuracy of the CUSIP numbers either as printed on the Notes or as contained in this Notice.
>
> The Trustee may periodically communicate with holders of the Notes through written notice of material events of a public nature of which the Trustee has knowledge. While the Trustee will endeavor to keep holders informed of major developments that affect their Notes, the Trustee does not intend to provide regular updates.
>
> Holders should not rely on the Trustee as their sole source of information. The Trustee makes no recommendations and gives no investment, legal, tax or other advice as to the above matters or as to the Notes generally.

9.8 Is a notice confidential or subject to the attorney-client or common interest privileges?

No. Notices transmitted by DTC are published on DTC's LENS system and are available to all participants, for retransmission to customers. Notices on LENS generally are widely available, and are sometimes even republished by participants or holders on wire services such as Bloomberg or Debtwire.

Communications, even private ones, between the indenture trustee and holders are not privileged except in certain limited instances, such as litigation in which there is a common interest. Notices, however, are never considered privileged communications.

9.9 Should an indenture trustee disclose non-public information in a notice?

No. Notices may only contain non-confidential, public information.

9.10 How do beneficial holders receive notices from the indenture trustee, and notices from an issuer or the bankruptcy court relating to an issuer's bankruptcy case?

Most beneficial holders hold their securities through a broker in street name and rely on their broker to transmit notices sent by the indenture trustee to DTC. Sometimes, although infrequently, retail holders hold certificated securities or are registered holders, to enable them to receive notices directly from the indenture trustee.

Beneficial holders do not automatically receive notices during a bankruptcy case unless they file a proof of right to record status under Fed. R. Bankr. P. 3003(d). Rule 3003(d), provides, in pertinent part:

> For the purposes of Rules 3017, 3018 and 3021 and for receiving notices, an entity who is not the record holder of the security may file a statement setting forth facts which entitle that entity to be treated as the record holder.

Fed. R. Bankr. P. 3003(d). Most beneficial holders do not file for record status under Rule 3003(d).

Institutional holders often maintain PACER (Public Access to Court Electronic Records) accounts as well as bankruptcy news subscriptions so as to monitor cases without having to identify their holdings publicly in a Fed. R. Bankr. P. 3003(d) filing.

Chapter 10. The Indenture Trustee's Pre-Bankruptcy Role

10.1 When the indenture trustee is informed that an issuer intends to file a chapter 11 petition, what steps should the indenture trustee take?

The answer varies case by case. In many instances, the indenture trustee will learn of an issuer's anticipated chapter 11 filing from holders who are in negotiations with the issuer regarding the terms of a proposed restructuring to be effectuated through a chapter 11 case.

Even if an issuer's anticipated chapter 11 filing is rumored, the indenture trustee's duties are limited to those specifically provided for in the indenture until an event of default has occurred.

10.2 Prior to a bankruptcy filing, does a bankruptcy restructuring negotiated by a group of holders with an issuer require the indenture trustee's involvement?

Not necessarily, but this varies case by case. Holder groups (commonly called "*ad hoc*" groups) will sometimes ask the indenture trustee to take certain actions in anticipation of the issuer's bankruptcy. Such actions may include notifying all holders of the formation of an *ad hoc* group, or the *ad hoc* group's retention of counsel; the entry into a confidentiality agreement by the indenture trustee; or retention of counsel or the professionals by the indenture trustee. The trustee's rights under the indenture encompass such actions following an event of default.

In the case of a secured indenture, the indenture trustee's consent may be needed for the entry into a proposed cash collateral order negotiated with the debtor in anticipation of a chapter 11 filing.

10.3 Should an indenture trustee notify all holders when some holders have signed confidentiality agreements with the issuer?

While this is within each indenture trustee's discretion, an indenture trustee will often notify holders that the issuer is requiring that holders who wish to receive confidential information (in connection with evaluating an issuer's restructuring proposal or the holders' recovery options) sign a confidentiality or non-disclosure agreement. The indenture trustee may, in a notice, indicate that holders who wish to enter into a confidentiality agreement in order to obtain confidential information from the issuer may contact the issuer directly.

10.4 May an indenture trustee sign a confidentiality agreement or non-disclosure agreement ("NDA")?

Following an event of default, the indenture trustee may sign a confidentiality agreement or NDA with the defaulting issuer, but is not obligated to do so. If an indenture trustee deems it reasonable and prudent to do so, it may sign a confidentiality agreement or NDA in connection with negotiations with the issuer or to review a restructuring proposal made to holders.

PRACTICE TIP

Confidentiality agreements signed by the indenture trustee should contain the following terms:

- The agreement should terminate on a date certain by which the issuer agrees to make all information public, either through a press release or public filing (usually the filing of a chapter 11 disclosure statement).
- The agreement must not preclude the indenture trustee from disclosing any information to regulators or auditors, or if required by law or court order.

- The agreement should not apply to information already known to the indenture trustee or obtained by the indenture trustee from an independent source.

10.5 May the indenture trustee provide confidential information to holders?

The indenture trustee may not disclose confidential information it obtains pursuant to a confidentiality agreement or NDA, except as permitted by the agreement. Further, the indenture trustee should not make selective disclosures of confidential information, whether or not it is contractually required to keep the information confidential. Securities regulations prohibit an issuer or others acting on its behalf from selectively disclosing material non-public information to holders or securities market professionals who may foreseeably trade on the information. 17 C.F.R. § 243.100. While it is not clear that an indenture trustee could be considered a person "acting on behalf" of an issuer, it is clear that the regulations prohibit the selective disclosure of sensitive information that may be used by some holders to trade in the securities.

When an issuer is providing confidential information to holders who have agreed not to trade in the securities under a confidentiality agreement providing for trading restrictions, the indenture trustee should request that the issuer offer all holders the same opportunity.

10.6 What are restricted holders?

Restricted holders are holders who have agreed not to trade in the securities, usually for a finite period of time, as a condition of receiving confidential or non-public information from or concerning an issuer. Holders become restricted usually in connection with examining or evaluating a potential transaction or restructuring.

PART IV

BANKRUPTCY

PART IV:

Bankruptcy

Chapter 11. The Indenture Trustee's Role Immediately After the Commencement of a Chapter 11 Case

11.1 How is a chapter 11 case commenced?

The debtor files a chapter 11 petition (Official Form 1) with the bankruptcy court, and the case is immediately and automatically commenced.

11.2 How does a chapter 11 filing by an issuer affect the indenture trustee and the holders of debt securities?

A chapter 11 filing dramatically affects the rights of the indenture trustee and the holders. Chapter 11 of the Bankruptcy Code stays the exercise of remedies against the debtor or its property, including the filing of law suits, except in bankruptcy court.

Chapter 11 allows an issuer, as a debtor in possession, the opportunity to completely restructure its balance sheet and capital structure. Subject to conditions and limitations in the Bankruptcy Code, the debtor may exchange its existing debt securities for new debt securities, new equity, cash, or a combination of debt, equity and/or cash. Holders can be forced to accept new securities with a value of much less than the par value of their existing securities. In some cases, the indenture and debt securities may be extinguished without any payment whatsoever, resulting in holders receiving nothing.

11.3 Does the indenture trustee have standing to appear in an issuer's chapter 11 case?

Yes. Bankruptcy Code § 1109 provides:

> . . . any indenture trustee[] may raise and may appear and be heard on any issue in a case under this chapter.

Bankruptcy Code § 1109(b).

11.4 What are "first day motions"?

First day motions refer to various papers and motions that are typically filed either at the same time as the chapter 11 petition or shortly thereafter. These include a first day affidavit or declaration which sets forth the factual background of the case. First day motions may also include a motion to approve cash management procedures (including use of bank accounts), a motion to pay employees, a motion to pay critical pre-petition vendors, a motion for joint administration of affiliated debtors, and a motion to approve use of cash collateral and/or to obtain debtor-in-possession financing on an interim basis.

First day motions are mostly administrative in nature, but occasionally can be substantive, if not case-determinative.

PRACTICE TIP

<u>Chapter 11 "First Day" Checklist for Indenture Trustee's Counsel</u>

1. Review docket and first day pleadings
2. Register for email notifications on ECF utilities, so as to receive email notifications of filings immediately
3. File a Notice of Appearance and Request for Service (as soon as possible)

4. If the debt securities are secured, review first day motions for issues affecting collateral, especially motions for use of cash collateral and/or for obtaining debtor in possession financing
5. If the debt securities are unsecured, review first day motions for issues affecting the holders
6. Prepare and file any objections that are warranted
7. If the debt securities are unsecured or under-secured:
   - Check the United States Trustee's website for the scheduling of a Committee formation meeting
   - Prepare the Committee questionnaire for submission to the United States Trustee
8. Prepare, for the indenture trustee's review, a notice to holders concerning the bankruptcy filing and the first day motions

Chapter 12. Creditors' Committees

12.1 What is a creditors' committee?

A creditors' committee (a "Committee") refers to an official unsecured creditors' committee appointed by the United States Trustee. The Committee is ordinarily chosen from holders of the seven largest unsecured claims of the kind represented by the Committee who are willing to serve. 11 U.S.C. §§ 1102(a)(b)(1).

A Committee is typically composed of and represents all major unsecured creditor groups, including trade creditors, unions and/or employees. A Committee provides advice and consent to the chapter 11 debtor in all aspects of the case.

Committees have the authority to investigate the debtor's financial condition and reorganization process (including reviewing its assets, liabilities, and operations) to determine its viability and reorganization options. Committees also investigate potential claims that could be asserted to benefit the estate and the creditors, such as transfers which occurred before bankruptcy and which could be challenged under the bankruptcy avoidance powers. In addition, Committees examine the strength of secured creditors' claims to collateral to uncover defects and set aside liens, in order to make such assets available as a source of recovery to unsecured creditors.

The chapter 11 plan is usually a product of negotiation between the debtor and the Committee, as well as other constituencies, including senior secured creditors.

12.2 What is the role of the indenture trustee with respect to a Committee in an issuer's chapter 11 case?

Where the debt securities issued under an indenture are unsecured, the role of the indenture trustee in a bankruptcy case includes service on the Committee as the representative of the holders collectively. A trustee under a secured indenture may also seek to serve on a Committee if the debt securities are undersecured and if the interests of the holders in the case are aligned with the general unsecured creditors.

12.3 What is the basis of the indenture trustee's authority to serve on a Committee?

Most indentures expressly provide that the indenture trustee shall be entitled to participate as a member, voting or otherwise, of any official committee of creditors appointed in the case of an issuer.

The indenture trustee's authority under the typical indenture broadly includes the right, if an event of default occurs and is continuing, to pursue any available remedy at law or in equity to collect the payment of principal or interest due to holders. Even in the absence of specific language authorizing the indenture trustee to serve on a Committee, the broad authority to pursue any available remedy can be read to include service on a Committee.

12.4 Why should an indenture trustee serve on a Committee?

A Committee may be the most significant, and sometimes the only, vehicle that debt security holders have to influence the formulation of a chapter 11 plan before it is filed. The indenture trustee's place on the Committee provides an important opportunity for holder interests to have a "seat at the table" in the Committee's negotiation of a plan.

Serving on the Committee gives the indenture trustee direct involvement in Committee decisions, including the selection of counsel and financial advisors for the Committee. Such selections can be critical in advancing the interests of unsecured creditors and, specifically, the debt security holders.

Indenture trustees will generally support the selection of advisors who are attuned to the objectives of the indenture trustee and the holders and who will not elevate the interests of another constituency on the Committee (such as unions or trade creditors) over those of the trustee and the holders.

In a case where the potential recovery to unsecured creditors is low, there is often a tension between and among the interests of holders (the "old, cold" debt), the trade creditors, and employees or unions. The holders may not be as invested in maintaining the debtor as a going concern if the recovery would be greater if the debtor's assets were sold either as a going concern or pursuant to a piecemeal liquidation. On the other hand, trade creditors and employees may favor a "stand alone" plan that preserves their contracts and ongoing business relationships with the debtor. Trade creditors and employees may oppose any sale scenario unless their contracts are assumed and assigned to a purchaser. Such conditions to a sale may depress the potential value to be realized in a sale and reduce holders' recovery.

Counsel with vested loyalties to groups other than holders or with preconceived notions as to the disposition of the case may not ultimately advance the interests of holders. The indenture trustee has only one vote on the Committee in its selection of counsel and advisors, but its voice is often an influential one because of its familiarity and experience with the Committee process.

Committee participation is consistent with the indenture trustee's standard of care, given that a prudent person would seek to join a Committee as a means of having an influence in the debtor's reorganization.

12.5 Is the indenture trustee required to seek appointment to the Committee?

Yes, it is generally required under the prudent person standard. As a matter of best practices, an indenture trustee for unsecured debt securities should apply to serve on the Committee unless there is a compelling reason not to.

Standard indentures provide that, if an event of default has occurred and is continuing, the indenture trustee shall exercise the rights and powers vested in it by the indenture and use the same degree of care and skill in its exercise as a prudent person would exercise or use under the circumstances in the conduct of such person's own affairs. Because of the important role of a Committee and its potential effect on the outcome of a chapter 11 case, a prudent person holding a large claim would seek to sit on a Committee.

PRACTICE TIP

The process that the United States Trustee employs to appoint a Committee varies region to region. Generally, the United States Trustee will send a questionnaire or application to the largest unsecured creditors as listed by the debtor in its initial bankruptcy filings. In many cases, the United States Trustee will schedule a meeting (called a "formation" or "organizational" meeting) of creditors at which the United States Trustee selects the members of the Committee.

Prior to the organizational meeting, the indenture trustee should submit, in addition to the questionnaire, a letter to United States Trustee setting forth the details of the debt securities which the indenture trustee represents, and providing the reasons why the indenture trustee should be considered for the Committee. These reasons may include:

- The need for holders to have representation on the Committee, including the size of their claims and the need for their support for any plan of reorganization to be approved
- The fact that the indenture trustee is the only representative of all holders, including retail holders who would otherwise be unrepresented
- The experience of the indenture trustee on Committees in similar cases

12.6 Is the indenture trustee entitled to compensation for serving on a Committee?

Yes, under the indenture the trustee is entitled to compensation and reimbursement of expenses for its services, including service on a Committee. The indenture trustee may charge for its extraordinary services at its standard hourly rates, as well as reimbursement of expenses, including the fees and expenses of professionals (counsel and, if necessary, financial advisors and consultants).

Committee members are entitled to reimbursement of expenses under an express Bankruptcy Code provision, but such provision does not include reimbursement of counsel fees. *See* 11 U.S.C. § 503(b)(3)(F).

12.7 How should the indenture trustee respond to a request by a holder or holders not to seek appointment to the Committee?

Sometimes an individual holder will urge the indenture trustee not to serve on the Committee, either out of concern that the appointment of the trustee may take up a slot on the Committee that may otherwise be given to the holder, or out of a desire to limit the fees and costs incurred by the trustee. While the indenture trustee should consider the views of holders, the indenture trustee should not refrain from seeking to serve on the Committee unless the request is made by a holder or holders which own 100% of the outstanding securities. The indenture trustee represents the entirety of holders collectively; on the other hand, an individual holder has no duty (fiduciary, contractual or otherwise) to any other holder and can only represent itself.

12.8 What are the risks to an indenture trustee in serving on a Committee?

The risks to the indenture trustee in serving on a Committee are remote. Several layers of legal protection are afforded to an indenture trustee insulating it from liability for its actions as a member of a Committee.

First, the Committee is entitled to retain counsel and financial advisors, all of whom must be paid by the issuer in the bankruptcy case. The Committee is entitled to obtain advice of counsel with respect to any action or inaction by the Committee.

Second, actions taken by the Committee are taken collectively, not individually. Committee sessions (including discussions and votes) are confidential, and only minimal minutes are kept. Therefore, asserting a claim against an individual member based on an action taken by the Committee would be difficult to establish or maintain.

Third, Committees and their members, including indenture trustees, are afforded a limited immunity for their activities as members of an official committee.

Fourth, Committee members generally receive exculpation for their actions in connection with their service on the Committee under a confirmed plan.

Fifth, indenture trustees may, and generally do, retain their own independent counsel to provide advice and recommendations. The Model Indenture provides that the indenture trustee may consult with counsel of its own selection and that the advice or opinion of counsel with respect to legal matters shall be full and complete protection from liability in respect of any action taken or not taken in good faith.

12.9 Should the indenture trustee disclose to holders matters discussed and information obtained through the Committee?

As a Committee member, an indenture trustee may not disclose confidential Committee matters. Moreover, information obtained through the Committee is often non-public information which should not be disclosed selectively. Only information that is available to all holders should be disclosed.

PRACTICE TIP

An indenture trustee on a Committee should require that the indenture trustee's counsel institute screening procedures to maintain the confidentiality of Committee information and to insulate such information from other personnel in counsel's firm, especially personnel who represent other creditors or parties in the case who are not on the Committee.

12.10 What should the indenture trustee do when the interests of holders conflict with the interests of other general unsecured creditors?

Quite often, debt securities are the largest unsecured claims in the case, as well as the largest claims represented by the Committee. Thus, the interests of the holders and that of the majority of general unsecured creditors are often one and the same. Occasionally, however, this is not the case. Consider, for example, a case in which the Committee is considering supporting a substantive consolidation which benefits the general creditors but dilutes the interest of the holders.

When the interests of holders and other unsecured creditors materially collide on a particular question, the indenture trustee should advocate the position of the holders during any Committee discussion on the question. If a vote is held on an action to be taken by the Committee, and if the interests of the holders run directly contrary to the interests of general unsecured creditors collectively, the indenture trustee may wish to consider abstaining from the vote. By abstaining the indenture trustee avoids placing itself in a position of either voting contrary to the interests of the holder it represents, or contrary to its role as a member of a Committee with fiduciary duties to unsecured creditors collectively.

12.11 Is the indenture trustee required or permitted to follow a direction by holders as to how to vote on a Committee matter, such as selection of counsel or financial advisors?

The indenture trustee is allowed, but not required, to follow such a direction. As further discussed in Chapter 4, the standard indenture provides that that the holders of a majority of the outstanding principal amount of the debt securities can direct the indenture trustee as to the conduct of any remedy or the exercise of any trust or power conferred on the trustee. For example, the Model Indenture provides:

> **Section 6.05. Control by Majority.**
>
> The Holders of a majority in Principal amount of the Securities may direct the time, method and place of conducting any proceeding for any remedy available to the Trustee or exercising any trust or power conferred on the Trustee. However, the Trustee may refuse to follow any direction that conflicts with law or this Indenture, is unduly prejudicial to the rights of other Securityholders, or would involve the Trustee in personal liability or expense for which the Trustee has not received a satisfactory indemnity.

Model Indenture § 6.05.

One threshold question is whether the direction as to a vote on a Committee matter constitutes the conduct of a proceeding, or the exercise of a trust or power. While service on a Committee is, certainly, consistent with the indenture trustee's standard of care in acting as a "prudent person" *In re Worldwide Direct, Inc.*, 334 B.R. 112, 131 (Bankr. D. Del 2005) (indenture trustee was prudent in acting as co-chair of creditors' committee), a vote on a Committee matter is not literally the conduct of a proceeding or the exercise of a trust or power.

Moreover, the indenture trustee, as a Committee member, has a fiduciary role with respect to the unsecured creditors collectively and must act in a manner consistent with that role. The indenture trustee may decline to follow a direction if it conflicts with law. If following the direction to cast a vote in a specific fashion collides with the indenture trustee's fiduciary role as a Committee member, the indenture trustee may decline to follow the direction.

The indenture trustee must also consider how following the direction may affect other, non-directing holders. Moreover, if the direction creates potential personal liability — for example, if it would subject the indenture trustee to claims for breach of fiduciary duty — the indenture trustee may decline to follow the direction.

Chapter 13. Proofs of Claim

13.1 What is a proof of claim?

A proof of claim is a document that a creditor must file with the bankruptcy court to register its claim in the case.

13.2 What constitutes a claim?

The word "claim" has a broad definition under the Bankruptcy Code.

Section 101(5) provides:

The term "claim" means—

> (A) right to payment, whether or not such right is reduced to judgment, liquidated, unliquidated, fixed, contingent, matured, unmatured, disputed, undisputed, legal, equitable, secured, or unsecured; or
>
> (B) right to an equitable remedy for breach of performance if such breach gives rise to a right to payment, whether or not such right to an equitable remedy is reduced to judgment, fixed, contingent, matured, unmatured, disputed, undisputed, secured, or unsecured.

11 U.S.C. § 101(5).

13.3 Who files the proof of claim with respect to debt securities?

The indenture trustee files the proof of claim with respect to all obligations owed under the indenture and the debt securities, including principal, interest, premium, and all other obligations. The indenture trustee's authority to file a proof of claim derives from numerous sources, including the Bankruptcy Code, Bankruptcy Rules, Trust Indenture Act, and indenture provisions.

1. Bankruptcy Code.

Section 501(a) of the Bankruptcy Code provides that an indenture trustee may file a proof of claim. The section states:

> A creditor or an indenture trustee may file a proof of claim.

2. Bankruptcy Rules.

Fed. R. Bankr. P. 3003(c)(5) tracks and clarifies Bankruptcy Code § 501(a):

> (5) Filing by Indenture Trustee[.] An indenture trustee may file a claim on behalf of all known or unknown holders of securities issued pursuant to the trust instrument under which it is trustee.

3. TIA.

In the case of TIA-qualified indentures, TIA § 317(a)(2) provides the indenture trustee with the authority to file proofs of claim or documents necessary to have the claim of the trustee recognized and allowed in any judicial proceeding involving the issuer.

TIA § 317(a) provides:

The indenture trustee shall be authorized: . . .

> (2) To file such proofs of claim and other papers or documents as may be necessary or advisable in order to have the claims of such trustee and of the indenture security holders allowed in any judicial proceedings

> relative to the obligor upon the indenture securities, its creditors, or its property[.]

4. The Indenture.

The standard indenture provides that the indenture trustee files the proof of claim on behalf of itself and the holders. Some typical language reads as follows:

> Trustee May File Proofs of Claim. The Trustee may file such proofs of claim, statements of interest and other papers or documents as may be necessary or advisable in order to have the claims of the Trustee (including any claim for reasonable compensation, expenses, disbursements and advances of the Trustee, including counsel, accountants, experts or such other professionals as the Trustee deems necessary, advisable or appropriate) and the holders allowed in any judicial proceedings relative to the Issuer, its creditors, or its property.

The above provision, which authorizes the indenture trustee to file a proof of claim, is among the express remedies under the indenture provided to the trustee. Even aside from this express language, the indenture trustee is given the broad right under the indenture to enforce remedies and collect amounts due after an event of default. Those enforcement rights encompass the filing of a proof of claim.

13.4 Is the indenture trustee the only party that can file a proof of claim for the debt securities issued under the indenture?

In subordinated notes indentures, the proof of claim authorization often includes not just the subordinated notes indenture trustee but also the senior notes indenture trustee. The rationale for this is that in some indentures, the senior and subordinated notes are *pari passu* as to the debtor, and the subordination is operative only as between the senior and subordinated holders themselves. In this scenario, the subordinated notes and senior notes are entitled to the same *pro rata* distribution from the debtor. The subordinated indenture requires however that if the senior notes have not been paid in full, any distribution made on account of the subordinated notes be paid over to the senior notes indenture trustee.

In an instance where the distribution from the estate is insufficient to pay the senior holders in full and thus the subordinated notes will not be entitled to retain any distribution it receives, the subordinated notes indenture trustee could conceivably forego the filing of a claim, especially if it involves incurring expense which does not benefit itself or the holders of the subordinated notes. Therefore, the indenture provision allowing the senior notes indenture trustee to file the claim on behalf of the subordinated notes is intended to ensure that the senior notes indenture trustee can preserve its right to distributions made on account of the subordinated notes.

If holders have claims against the debtor that do not arise from the indenture, these must be filed individually by the holders.

13.5 What are the contents of a proof of claim?

Fed. R. Bankr. P. 3001(a) requires that proofs of claim be submitted in the official form. If the claim is based on a writing, the proof of claim must include the writing. Fed. R. Bankr. P. 3001(c)(1). Rather than attaching voluminous documents, a creditor may summarize the supporting documents and make them available on request. *See* Official Form 410.

PRACTICE TIP

An indenture trustee's proof of claim should include:

- A breakdown of principal outstanding and interest accrued as of the petition date
- A reservation of rights to assert post petition, administrative claims
- An assertion of claims for amounts not yet determined, including claims for breach of the indenture, and compensation and indemnification claims
- A copy of the indenture and any other operative documents on which the claim is based

13.6 What is the deadline for filing a claim?

The deadline for filing a claim in a chapter 7 or chapter 13 case is 90 days after the first date set for the meeting of creditors under 11 U.S.C. § 341(a). Fed. R. Bankr. P. 3002(e). In a chapter 11 case, the deadline is generally set by the bankruptcy court upon motion filed by the debtor in possession.

13.7 Where is a claim filed?

A proof of claim must be filed in the bankruptcy court where the case is pending. Fed. R. Bankr. P. 3002(b) and 5005.

In a chapter 11 case, the manner of filing and the precise place of filing are set forth in a notice and order setting the bar date for filing proofs of claim entered by the bankruptcy court. To the extent this is not specifically addressed in the bar date order and notice, the bankruptcy court's local rules should be consulted.

Generally, claims may be filed directly with the bankruptcy court, although in large cases, the debtor may be directed by the bankruptcy court to retain a claims agent, so as to reduce the administrative burden on the bankruptcy clerk's office. 28 U.S.C. § 156(c). The bar date order will direct the place of filing (*i.e.,* the bankruptcy court or the claims agent), as well as other claim filing procedures.

In many jurisdictions, including the Southern District of New York and the District of Delaware, claims may be filed electronically on the court's electronic case filing ("ECF") system, except where a claims agent is appointed. Some claims agents also have procedures for electronic filing.

13.8 Must a proof of claim be signed?

Yes, a proof of claim must be signed by the creditor or an authorized person. Fed. R. Bankr. P. 3001 (b).

13.9 Who is authorized to sign a proof of claim?

Strictly speaking, the requirement that claims be filed by the creditor or an authorized person means that a proof of claim must be signed either by an individual who has authority to sign on behalf of the creditor, whether on internal authority (a person with signing authority within a corporate trust department), or an agent or professional who holds a power of attorney.

While, of course, it is advisable to adhere to the signatory authority requirements, in practice, the requirement is loosely applied. Every proof of claim must have a signature, but the authority of the signatory is not often probed or examined by the debtor, other creditors, or the bankruptcy court. Claims are rarely, if ever, rejected or objected to simply on the basis of the person who signed the claim. For example, if the claim is signed by a lawyer who represents the indenture trustee but does not hold a power of attorney, or by an employee of the indenture trustee who is not a senior trust officer with internal signing authority, this will rarely, if ever, lead to an objection.

13.10 Who should sign a proof of claim on behalf of the indenture trustee?

The signatory should have knowledge of the claim and apparent authority to sign the claim. In the event the claim is objected to by the debtor or another creditor, the signatory may be deposed, and he or she will be questioned under oath as to his or her personal knowledge of the claim.

13.11 Should counsel sign a proof of claim?

Lawyers should not sign a proof of claim, except in an emergency when there is no other way to timely file the claim. Counsel's signing a claim may waive the attorney-client privilege as to the contents of the claim. *See, e.g., Schmidt v. Rodriguez (In re Rodriguez)*, No. 10-70606, 2013 WL 2450925, at * 3-4 (Bankr. S.D. Tex. June 5, 2013). Also, as noted above, the signatory may be deposed if a claim is objected to. By signing the claim, the lawyer may become a witness, and he or she (and possibly his or her firm) may be precluded from representing the indenture trustee in connection with a dispute regarding the claim.

13.12 Do holders need to file claims for principal and interest?

No. The indenture trustee's proof of claim asserts the principal and interest claims of all of the holders collectively. Bar date orders often contain language expressly stating that the holders are not required to file a claim for obligations arising under the indenture, and that the indenture trustee shall file one proof of claim on behalf of all of the holders.

Holders of debt securities will sometimes file claims as a protective matter. The claims filed by individual holders are eventually expunged to the extent that the indenture trustee has filed a proof of claim.

13.13 What other provisions of a bar date order may affect the indenture trustee?

The bar date order usually include provisions specifically applicable to the indenture trustees. For example, some bar date orders provide that the indenture trustee need file only a single claim in the jointly administered, non-substantively consolidated cases of several debtor obligors and guarantors. In the absence of such a provision (or stipulation providing that a single claim may be filed), the indenture trustee must file a separate claim in the case of each debtor that is an obligor or guarantor under the indenture. It is important to note that failure to file a claim in the individual case of a guarantor or obligor could result in a waiver or forfeiture of the claim against that debtor.

13.14 How should an original issue discount be handled in a proof of claim?

An original issue discount (an "OID") security is discounted in the original issuance and issued at a price lower than par. The amount outstanding on the maturity date is the par value, not the original issue price. An OID is in essence interest that is payable upon maturity of the security.

An OID is treated in most respects as interest. Under the Bankruptcy Code, claims for unmatured interest are not allowable. 11 U.S.C. § 502(b)(2). The total discount is amortized over the term of the securities, and the amount accrued prior to the bankruptcy petition is allowable as a pre-petition claim. *In re Residential Capital, LLC,* 501 B.R. 549, 589 (Bankr. S.D.N.Y. 2013).

An OID can also be created in face value exchanges or fair value exchanges done in connection with a restructuring. At least one court has held that such an OID is allowable in a bankruptcy case notwithstanding Bankruptcy Code § 501(b)(2). *LTV Corp. v. Valley Fidelity Bank & Trust Co. (In re Chateaugay Corp.)*, 961 F.2d 378, 380 (2d Cir. 1992).

PRACTICE TIP

Because the law surrounding treatment of an OID has evolved and may continue to evolve, the treatment of an OID in a bankruptcy is not definitively settled. Thus, the preferred course of action by an indenture trustee is to include the entire OID amount in the proof of claim. The assertion of the full OID amount, however, may lead to a claims objection, which the indenture trustee may defend or resolve, as discussed in Chapter 14.

13.15 May a proof of claim be filed even if there is no default?

Yes, the definition of claim under the Bankruptcy Code is broad and includes all obligations under an indenture even if there has been no default. Section 101(5)(A) of the Bankruptcy Code provides:

> (5) the term "claim" means —
>
> (A) a right to payment, whether or not such right is reduced to judgment, liquidated, unliquidated, fixed, contingent, matured, unmatured, disputed, undisputed, legal, equitable, secured, or unsecured[.]

Bankruptcy Code § 101(5)(A).

13.16 Should the proof of claim include the entire principal amount outstanding, even if the indenture trustee did not issue a notice of acceleration prior to bankruptcy?

Yes. Under Bankruptcy Code § 101(5)(A), a claim includes all amounts that arise prior to bankruptcy, whether matured or unmatured. Thus, the proof of claim should include all obligations arising under the indenture, whether or not due and payable, and whether or not a contractual acceleration has occurred.

13.17 What should be included in a proof of claim with respect to a secured indenture?

In addition to the contents that are required in a proof of claim with respect to an unsecured indenture, there are several additional requirements with respect to a secured claim.

First, the claim must include proof of perfection of the security interest. Fed. R. Bankr. P. 3001(d).

Second, the collateral must be described. The proof of claim form (Official Form 410) requires a statement as to the value of the collateral and the amount of the claim which is unsecured. Under the Bankruptcy Code, a creditor's claim is deemed to be a secured claim to the extent of the value of the creditor's interest in collateral, and an unsecured claim to the extent of any deficiency. 11 U.S.C. § 506(c).

The value of the collateral may be undetermined or unknown, and thus the amount of the claim which is unsecured is also undetermined or unknown. A common practice is to indicate both the value of the collateral and the amount of the deficiency claim as undetermined. This retains enables the indenture trustee to argue for a specific collateral valuation and deficiency amount at a later point in the bankruptcy case as facts develop, without prematurely locking in a position.

PRACTICE TIP

The indenture trustee's proof of claim should assert and preserve all claims under the indenture, including claims that may be incurred post petition. An example of language that encompasses such claims is the following:

> The Issuer is also liable under the terms of the Indenture for certain unliquidated amounts including the Indenture Trustee's fees, expenses, disbursements,

indemnification, and advances (including, for the avoidance of doubt, compensation, fees, expenses and disbursements of the Indenture Trustee's agents and counsel), which have been incurred and continue to be incurred during the case), which each Issuer is obligated to pay under, *inter alia*, section 7.07 of the Indenture, and which are entitled to priority payment pursuant to sections 7.07 and 6.08 of the Indenture.

The Indenture Trustee reserves its right to assert any and all other claims arising under the Indenture and/ or the Notes, including any premiums, post petition interest, interest payable on overdue interest at the rates provided in the Notes and the Indenture, and damages for breaches of any covenant, representation, warranty or any other provision of the Indenture.

The Indenture Trustee expressly reserves the right to amend or supplement this proof of claim for any reason, including to update the statement of the amounts due, or for any other purpose for which a proof of claim filed in this proceeding could be amended, or to file additional proofs of claim for additional claims, including, without limitation, administrative expense claims, unsecured claims, claims against other debtors whose cases are being jointly administered with that of the Issuer, and all other claims, at law or in equity, arising prior to, on or after the Petition Date, or to amend or supplement this proof of claim.

13.18 Does a proof of claim need to be stated in United States Dollars?

An order setting a bar date for filing a proof of claim usually will contain language stating that the claim must be filed in United States Dollars ("USD"). However, section 501 of the Bankruptcy Code does not specifically require that a claim be filed in USD, nor does Fed. R. Bankr. P. 3001. Nevertheless, claims filed in currency other than USD will normally draw objections, and the amount of the claim ultimately allowed will be the amount in USD as of the bankruptcy petition date. This is consistent with the language of section 502(b) of the Bankruptcy Code, which provides that if an objection to a proof of claim is made:

> … the court, after notice and a hearing, shall determine the amount of such claim in lawful currency of the United States as of the date of the filing of the petition, and shall allow such claim in such amount….

11 U.S.C. § 502(b). Section 502(b) has been construed as freezing a claim under an agreement denominated in foreign currency to the amount in USD calculated at the exchange rate on the date of the bankruptcy petition. *In re Global Power Equipment Group Inc.*, Nos. 06-11045(BLS), 1911, 2191, 2213, 2008 WL 435197, at *4-5 (Bankr. D. Del., Feb. 14, 2008), *aff'd*, 400 B.R. 17 (D. Del. 2009).

13.19 Why does it matter what currency the claim is asserted in?

Due to currency fluctuations, exchange rates vary from time to time. The value of a claim which arises in one currency but is paid in a different currency could swing dramatically if the exchange rate between the two currencies changes between the filing of the petition and the date of distribution. For example, if at the time the bankruptcy petition is filed the euro-USD exchange rate is €1/$1.10, and a year later, when the distribution is made, the euro-USD exchange rate is €1/$1.35, then a claim for €500 would equal $550 on the petition date, but a distribution of $550 a year later (at the €1/$1.35 exchange rate) would only be worth €407,41.

Section 502(b) is intended to fix the amounts in USD as of the date of the petition, regardless of currency fluctuations.

13.20 What provisions in an indenture relate to claims arising under a non-US currency?

Certain provisions relating to payment in a non-US currency, known as currency indemnification provisions, are often found in indentures under which euro debt securities (securities issued in a currency other that of the issuer's) are issued. An example of such a provision is as follows:

> Any amount with respect to the Notes received or recovered in a currency other than euro, whether as a result of, or the enforcement of, a judgment or order of a court of any jurisdiction, in the winding-up or dissolution of the Issuer or any Guarantor or otherwise by any Holder of a Note or by the Trustee, in respect of any sum expressed to be due to it from the Issuer or any Guarantor will only constitute a discharge to the Issuer or any Guarantor to the extent of the euro amount which the recipient is able to purchase with the amount so received or recovered in that other currency on the date of that receipt or recovery (or, if it is not practicable to make that purchase on that date, on the first date on which it is practicable to do so).

> If that euro amount is less than the euro amount expressed to be due to the recipient or the Trustee under the Notes, the Issuer and each Guarantor will indemnify such recipient and/or the Trustee against any loss sustained by it as a result. In any event, the Issuer and each Guarantor will indemnify the recipient and/or the trustee against the cost of making any such purchase. ....This indemnity shall constitute a separate and independent obligation from the Issuer's and each Guarantor's other obligations, shall give rise to a separate and independent cause of action, shall apply irrespective of any waiver granted by any Holder of a Note or the Trustee (other than a waiver of the indemnities set out herein) and will continue in full force and effect despite any other judgment, order, claim or proof for a liquidated amount in respect of any sum due under any Note or to the Trustee. For the purposes of determining the amount in a currency other than euro, such amount shall be determined using the Exchange Rate then in effect.

Such an indemnification provision provides that the issuer will indemnify the indenture trustee for the loss caused by payment being made in a currency different from that required under the indenture. This indemnity constitutes a separate and independent obligation from the issuer's other obligations under the indenture, and give rise to a separate and independent cause of action.

The enforceability of a currency indemnification in a bankruptcy case is not free from doubt. There is no definitive authority on the allowability of a currency indemnification indemnity claim under the Bankruptcy Code.

PRACTICE TIP

Where an indenture provides that payment be made in a non-US currency and contains a currency indemnification, the proof of claim should specifically include a claim under the currency indemnification provision, including the difference in the value of the claim due to currency fluctuation between the bankruptcy filing and the distribution, as well as any costs or fees incurred in making the currency exchange.

13.21 Where one entity serves as indenture trustee and also acts in another capacity in connection with the debt securities, should it file a claim in each capacity?

Generally speaking, yes. For example, in a transaction where a company is obligated under more than one tranche of secured debt (*e.g.*, first priority notes and second priority notes, or first priority bank loans and first priority notes under an indenture), there is generally a collateral agency agreement under which a collateral agent holds the security interest in the collateral on behalf of all of the secured creditors. Typically there is also an intercreditor agreement (either in the collateral agency agreement or in a separate agreement) which governs the rights to the collateral among the parties to the agreement. The indenture trustee under a secured indenture might also serve as collateral agent.

The right to file a proof of claim on behalf of the debt security holders is vested expressly in the indenture trustee under the indenture, as well as bankruptcy law and, where applicable, the TIA. However the collateral agent may have separate rights to fees, expenses and indemnification. Further, the right to exercise remedies against the collateral is arguably a claim under the broad definition of 11 U.S.C.

§ 101(5). For these reasons, a collateral agent may decide to file a protective proof of claim. This does not supplant the need for the indenture trustee to file a secured claim under the relevant indenture.

13.22 Aside from the collateral agent situation, are there other situations where the indenture trustee should file claims in more than one capacity?

Yes, there are a number of other situations in which claims in more than one capacity may need to be filed, for example, trust preferred securities or other hybrid securities, and other non-traditional or specialized forms of financing.

One example is a leveraged lease or equipment trust certificate arrangement. In such arrangements, securities (in the form of notes or certificates) are issued under an indenture by an owner trust which finances the purchase of equipment with the proceeds of the notes or certificates. The owner trust leases the equipment to the obligor/lessee, and assigns or grants a security interest in its rights as lessor under the lease to the trustee under the indenture. The documents typically provide that upon a default the indenture trustee may exercise all the rights of the owner trust under the lease. Thus, in a bankruptcy of the obligor/lessee, the indenture trustee will file a claim or claims under the lease (including pre-petition claims, rejection or stipulated loss value claims, and/or administrative claims).

If the trustee has potential claims under other instruments in the transaction (for example, under a participation agreement or indemnification agreement), the trustee should file separate claims for those as well.

13.23 What are trust preferred securities ("TruPS")?

Trust preferred securities ("TruPS") are hybrid securities, which have attributes of both equity and debt. They have been frequently used by bank holding companies because they are treated as equity for regulatory purposes and as debt for tax purposes.

In a TruPS structure, the obligor (generally a bank holding company), issues subordinated debentures to a special purpose subsidiary trust. The trust issues certificates to investors, and the proceeds of the certificates are lent by the trust to the parent/obligor, which guarantees the repayment of the certificates to the extent payments are made by the obligor to the trust.

13.24 How are claims filed with respect to TruPS?

Under most TruPS, the trustee holds claims against the obligor under subordinated debt securities, as well as under the guarantee. The preferred practice is to file separate claims, one in connection with each capacity or instrument. While the claims both relate to a single financing transaction and are part of one integrated agreement, the claims arise under different documents and are asserted by the trustee in two separate capacities (as indenture trustee for the subordinated debentures and as guarantee trustee). In such circumstances, caution dictates that separate claims be filed.

Chapter 14. Claims Objections

14.1 What is an objection to a claim?

Under section 502 of the Bankruptcy Code, a claim for which a proof of claim is filed is allowed unless a party in interest objects. 11 U.S.C. § 502(a). Fed. R. Bankr. P. 3007 requires that objections be made in writing, filed with the bankruptcy court, and served on the claimant at least 30 days prior to a hearing on the objection. An objection to a proof of claim may also be included in an adversary proceeding. Fed. R. Bankr. P. 3007(b).

14.2 Who can object to the indenture trustee's claim?

Any party in interest may file an objection. Bankruptcy Code § 502(a). Parties in interest include the debtor, creditor or equity holder. Bankruptcy Code § 1109 provides, in pertinent part:

> (b) A party in interest, including the debtor, the trustee, a creditors' committee, an equity security holders' committee, a creditor, an equity security holder, or any indenture trustee, may raise and may appear and be heard on any issue in a case under this chapter.

The interpretation of the term "party in interest" is very broad. At least one court, however, has held that certificate holders in a commercial mortgage backed security ("CMBS") are not parties in interest in a chapter 11 case of a CMBS borrower, because the certificate holders have no direct relationship or privity with the borrower/debtor. *In re Innkeepers USA Trust*, 448 B.R. 131, 141-42 (Bankr. S.D.N.Y. 2011).

The Securities and Exchange Commission, while not technically a party in interest, also has the right to be heard on any matter in a chapter 11 case. Bankruptcy Code § 1109(a).

14.3 What kind of objections are made to an indenture trustee's claim?

Some typical objections include those challenging:

- The calculation of principal and interest
- Post petition interest, including interest accruing on the petition date
- An OID, in whole or in part
- Default interest
- Indenture trustee's fees and expenses (including challenges to the reasonableness of the fees and expenses)
- Claims based on subsidiary or affiliate guarantees (on the grounds that the guarantees were fraudulent conveyances)
- Make-whole premiums

In the case of a secured claim, objections are sometimes based on challenges to the indenture trustee's secured status, including challenges under Bankruptcy Code § 506 based on the value of collateral, or the validity or perfection of liens.

14.4 What are the indenture trustee's duties with respect to defending objections?

The indenture trustee's duty with respect to responding to an objection is defined by the prudent person standard. The indenture trustee has the duty either to defend or resolve the objection, depending on which would be prudent. However, the trustee is not required to expend its own funds or subject itself to potential liability in the process.

14.5 Can the indenture trustee settle or compromise an objection to its claim in a bankruptcy case?

Yes, the indenture trustee may settle an objection to its claim, provided certain requirements are met. If the compromise changes or affects the holders' rights to, or ability to recover, principal or interest, the indenture trustee's authority is subject to certain requirements, conditions, and procedures, including notice to holders and an opportunity to object. *In re Delta Airlines, Inc.*, 370 B.R. 537 (Bankr. S.D.N.Y. 2007), *aff'd*, 374 B.R. 516 (S.D.N.Y 2007), *aff'd*, 309 Fed. App'x 455 (2d Cir. 2009).

The indenture trustee's authority to settle a claim is inherent in its power to file the claim in the first instance. *Id.*, at 548.

14.6 Does the anti-impairment provision in section 316(b) of the TIA prevent a modification of the holders' rights, including the amount of the holders' claims, in a bankruptcy?

No. The anti-impairment provisions in section 316(b) of the TIA, and the language tracking these provisions in most indentures, do not prevent holders' claims from being restructured in a bankruptcy proceeding. Section 316(b) of the TIA provides:

> Notwithstanding any other provision of the indenture to be qualified, the right of any holder of any indenture security to receive payment of the principal of and interest on such indenture security, on or after the respective due dates expressed in such indenture security, or to institute suit for the enforcement of any such payment on or after such respective dates, shall not be impaired or affected without the consent of such holder, except as to a postponement of an interest payment consented to as provided in paragraph (2)

> of subsection (a) of this section, and except that such indenture may contain provisions limiting or denying the right of any such holder to institute any such suit, if, and to the extent that, the institution or prosecution thereof, or the entry of judgment therein would, under applicable law, result in the surrender, impairment, waiver, or loss of the lien of such indenture upon any property subject to such lien.

In *Delta Air Lines, Inc.*, the United States Bankruptcy Court for the Southern District of New York wrote:

> First, it is an oft-repeated premise of the Objectors' position on this motion that they cannot be deprived of their contractual right to 100% of their entitlement to principal interest under the Indenture without their consent, and they do not consent. What is ignored is the fact that this is a bankruptcy case, and whether the Settlement is approved by this Court or not, the Bondholders including Objectors are not going to receive 100% of the amount to which they are entitled under the Indenture.

Id., at 541.

In *Delta Airlines, Inc.*, the court explained that the anti-impairment language does not apply to, and does not prevent, a modification of the holders' claims that occurs by operation of the Bankruptcy Code:

> [The anti-impairment provision of the indenture] is not concerned with default or bankruptcy or other events beyond the control of . . . the Bond Trustee — it relates to consensual modifications of the Indenture and the Agreement. We are not concerned here

> with a "supplemental indenture" (section 12.03) or amendments of the agreement or guaranty with or without consent of the owners (sections 12.06, 12.07), and those provisions are simply irrelevant here. The impairment which the Objectors complain of results not from any agreement of the Bond Trustee, but from operation of the Bankruptcy Code and the simple economic fact that this insolvent debtor cannot pay its creditors unimpaired.

Id. at 546-47.

14.7 What process must an indenture trustee follow in settling an objection to a proof of claim?

As a procedural matter, a dispute with respect to a proof of claim can be settled and compromised either through a motion to approve a settlement filed by the debtor under Fed. R. Bankr. P. 9019, or a chapter 11 plan.[7] Both require notice to holders with an opportunity to object. The indenture trustee may negotiate a proposed settlement, but the approval of the settlement (whether contained in a motion under Fed. R. Bankr. P. 9019, or pursuant to a chapter 11 plan) will be conditioned upon formal notice to holders with an opportunity to file an objection with the bankruptcy court. In order for their claims to be compromised under a chapter 11 plan, the holders must also be given the opportunity to vote to accept or reject the plan. Any settlement negotiated by the indenture trustee should also be subject to the right of the indenture trustee to terminate the settlement if directed to do so by holders with a majority of the outstanding securities.

The indenture trustee's decision to enter into a settlement of disputed claims is governed by the prudent person standard — the same standard applicable to its decision whether or not to defend objections to the claim. Some of the considerations that the indenture trustee often takes into account include the cost of litigation and the likelihood that such costs will be paid via the indenture trustee's charging lien (thereby reducing the recovery of holders), the merits of the claim, and the chances of prevailing in litigation.

PRACTICE TIP

<u>The indenture trustee's roadmap before entering into a settlement or compromise of claims under the indenture</u>

1. **Assessment:** Obtain an assessment from counsel as to the strengths and weaknesses of the claims, the likelihood of prevailing, the difficulty of collection or recovery, and the time, costs and risks of litigation.
2. **Notice:** Engage in a full communication process with holders, including providing notice to holders of the dispute and issues presented, and arranging conference calls in which all holders are invited to participate.
3. **Advice of Counsel:** Obtain the written recommendation of counsel as to the course of action to be taken, including whether to enter into a settlement.
4. **Decision:** Internal review and approval of the decision to enter into a settlement.
5. **Formal notice and approval:** Any settlement must be conditioned on bankruptcy court approval (either via a motion under Fed. R. Bankr. P. 9109 or a chapter 11 plan for which holders' votes are properly solicited), upon notice to all holders and the opportunity of holders to object.

PRACTICE TIP

An order approving a settlement entered into by the indenture trustee of any dispute or claim to which the indenture trustee is a party should, ideally, provide that:

1. Adequate and sufficient notice was given to all holders.
2. The settlement is fair and reasonable to the holders.
3. The agreement is consistent with the indenture trustee's rights, duties and powers under the indenture.
4. In entering into the settlement the indenture trustee is acting as a prudent person in the discharge of its duties under the indenture.
5. The indenture trustee and its representatives are released from liability to the holders for any claim relating to the settlement, and the holders are enjoined from pursuing litigation against the indenture trustee and its representatives.
6. The settlement and the order approving it are binding on all holders.
7. The settlement agreement is approved, and the indenture trustee and the debtor are authorized to enter into the settlement.

Some bankruptcy courts will decline to include all of these provisions (especially #2-5) in an order, even with a factual record supporting the findings, as they may view such provisions as unnecessary to the court's approval of a settlement and beyond the scope of the court's power. Other bankruptcy courts, however, will include these provisions based on the broad authority granted to the bankruptcy court under Bankruptcy Code § 105.

Chapter 15. Payment of Indenture Trustee's Fees and Expenses

15.1 When the issuer files for bankruptcy, how can an indenture trustee ensure that it is compensated for the fees and expenses it incurs during the case?

This is one of the most controversial questions in the area of indenture trustee representation. Indeed, there is no other question as to which the answers are more murky or ambiguous. The answers are not clear cut because:

> (1) The Bankruptcy Code does not squarely address the payment of indenture trustees' fees and expenses.
>
> (2) The case law is not well developed and has not provided any clear pathway for an indenture trustee to obtain payment directly from a debtor's estate.

The most favorable outcome for the indenture trustee and the holders is for the indenture trustee's fees and expenses to be paid in cash pursuant to a chapter 11 plan — in essence as an administrative expense in the case. This benefits both the holders and the indenture trustee because it avoids the exercise of the indenture trustee's charging lien against the plan distributions being made by the debtor on account of the debt securities.

Unfortunately, the indenture trustee's right to be paid in this manner has not been definitively settled by the courts. There is no clear or controlling case law holding that indenture trustees' fees and expenses are entitled to administrative expense treatment. In fact, there are a few cases, including a decision by the United States District Court for the Southern District of New York, that have denied such treatment. *See Davis v. Elliot Mgmt. Corp.* (*In re Lehman Bros. Holdings Inc.*), 508 B.R. 283, 287-88 (S.D.N.Y. 2014). Nevertheless, indenture trustees' fees historically have been paid in the majority of cases, most often through a negotiated treatment under a plan.

Obtaining payment is often driven more by practical, rather than legal, considerations, such as, for example, the parties' desire to reach a global agreement, a dynamic in which payment of advisor's fees and expenses is a "deal point." In many large cases, the indenture trustee's fees and expenses are such a small fraction of the overall fees and expenses that they are regarded as a "rounding error."

While they may pale in comparison to the overall professional fees in a chapter 11 case, the indenture trustee's fees and expenses can be substantial. Indenture trustees typically serve on Committees, which can involve hundreds of hours on the part of the indenture trustee and its counsel.

15.2 Do the fees and expenses need to be reasonable, and if so, who is the arbiter of reasonableness?

Yes, the fees and expenses must be reasonable. The Model Indenture provides for "reasonable" fees and expenses. Some indentures do not contain this qualifier. However, the Securities and Exchange Commission has asserted in a number of bankruptcy cases that any fees paid by a debtor pursuant to a plan must be approved by the court as reasonable under section 1129(a)(4) of the Bankruptcy Code. While arguably this does not apply to fees and expenses paid via the indenture trustee's exercise of its charging lien, in many cases the fees and expenses are paid directly by the debtor — essentially as if they were administrative expenses — in addition to, and not deducted from, the distributions to holders. The prevailing view is that, based on bankruptcy law as well as the language of most indentures, indenture trustees' fees and expenses that are paid by a debtor's estate are subject to a reasonableness standard.

The harder question is: who is the arbiter of reasonableness? Most chapter 11 plans that provide for payment of the fees and expenses of the indenture trustee also provide that the bankruptcy court will resolve any disputes regarding the reasonableness of the fees. On the other hand, if the fees are not being paid directly by the estate, but are being satisfied by the exercise of the charging lien, the bankruptcy court lacks jurisdiction over the issue of reasonableness or the appropriateness of the exercise of the charging lien. The distributions, once paid to the indenture trustee, are not property of the debtor's bankruptcy estate.

It is not clear whether an individual holder has the right to pursue a claim against the indenture trustee to disgorge allegedly unreasonable fees. While such an action might arguably require a threshold percentage of holders under the indenture's "no action" provisions, any requirement of instructing the trustee to pursue the action would be futile — and thus would be excused — because the indenture trustee could never be expected to bring a claim against itself. *See, e.g., Royal Park Investments SA/NV v. HSBC Bank USA, N.A.*, Nos. 14-cv-8175(SAS), 14-cv-9366(SAS), 14-cv-10101(SAS), 2015 WL 3466121, at *10 (S.D.N.Y. June 1, 2015).

15.3 What is the basis of an indenture trustee's entitlement to receive payment for its services and expenses during a chapter 11 proceeding?

There is no definitive or even majority view as to the basis for this entitlement. There are several theories of reimbursement that are typically asserted, but not every theory will be appropriate in an individual case. Obtaining payment involves careful strategy, developed on a case-by-case basis.

15.4 What legal theories are asserted by indenture trustees seeking compensation in a bankruptcy case?

The principal legal theories are, in summary, the following:

1. Administrative expense

Section 503(b) of the Bankruptcy Code provides that the bankruptcy court may allow administrative expenses for, among other things, the actual, necessary costs and expenses of preserving the estate. The administrative expense theory, while the most straightforward rationale, has proved to be the most controversial, and is widely discredited.

2. Indemnification

The indenture provides that the issuer indemnify the trustee for all fees, expenses, costs, and liabilities. The challenge in asserting this theory is that a number of cases hold that an indemnification claim under a contract entered into prior to the bankruptcy case is not entitled to administrative expense priority status but is, at best, a pre-petition claim. However, if the debtor's estate is solvent, the priority of the indemnification claim is less important because, in a solvent estate, pre-petition claims are likely to be paid in full.

A few courts have upheld the right of an unsecured creditor to fees and expenses that are recoverable under a valid contract as a matter of state law. In *Ogle v. Fidelity & Deposit Co. of Maryland,* 586 F.3d 143, 145-46 (2d Cir. 2009, the court held that the Bankruptcy Code does not prohibit an unsecured creditor from collecting post petition fees to which it is entitled under a contract enforceable under state law. The court cited *Travelers Cas. & Sur. Co. of America v. Pacific Gas & Elec. Co.*, 549 U.S. 443, 449 (2007), as supporting its reasoning, as well as cases upholding such claims, including *In re SNTL Corp.*, 571 F.3d 826, 839-45 (9th Cir. 2009); and *Martin v. Bank of Germantown (In re Martin),* 761 F.2d 1163, 1168 (6th Cir. 1985), but noted cases in other jurisdictions disallowing such claims. *See Adams v. Zimmerman*, 73 F.3d 1164, 1177 (1st Cir. 1996); *In re Waterman*, 248 B.R. 567, 573 (8th Cir. BAP 2000). The same rationale applies to an indenture trustee's entitlement to its fees and expenses under the compensation and indemnification provisions of the indenture, a contract which is enforceable as a matter of state contract law. A related but more obscure argument is that an indenture trustee is entitled to its fees and expenses as a trustee qualified under the TIA.

Ogle and the cases it relied upon suggest that the fees and expenses are allowable as a general unsecured claim rather than as an administrative expense. A rationale exists, however, to treat indemnification claims under an indenture differently from other contractual claims. An indemnification claim is a continuing obligation under an indenture arising from the indenture trustee's ongoing role as the representative of the debt securities. Unlike other creditors with contracts having provisions for recovery of fees, the indenture trustee does not have a choice as to whether to bring or defend litigation under the indenture or to continue to act as trustee during the bankruptcy case.

3. Executory contract

Under an executory contract, the obligations of both parties — the debtor and the counterparty — continue until the contract is rejected. *See* 11 U.S.C. § 365. If the indenture is an executory contract, the debtor's obligations under all indenture provisions (including those requiring it to pay the trustee's fees and expenses) continue until the indenture is rejected and discharged. Moreover, until the indenture is rejected, the indenture trustee is required to provide ongoing services which benefit the issuer — including serving as the representative of the holders collectively in a bankruptcy. Without an indenture trustee, a debtor would be faced with claims from hundreds or even thousands of holders, creating a huge administrative burden on the estate. Under the executory contract theory, the debtor is liable for the value of the services rendered by the indenture trustee until the indenture is rejected and discharged.

4. Charging lien

Under a typical indenture, the trustee has a charging lien which secures the payment of the trustees' fees, expenses and indemnification claims. The charging lien attaches to distributions made by the debtor under the plan. The indenture trustee's exercise of its charging lien does not require the approval or agreement of the debtor or the holders, but it does require that funds are actually available to the indenture trustee, either from a distribution from the debtor, the liquidation of collateral, or reserve funds held by the indenture trustee. Absent funds or property, there is nothing for the charging lien to attach to. Thus, the utility of the charging lien is limited to cases in which there are actually funds on which the charging lien can be exercised. In a case involving an unsecured indenture where the debtor is deeply insolvent and there are no funds distributable to the holders, there will be no funds on which the indenture trustee can exercise the charging lien.

5. Necessity doctrine

Many courts have authorized the debtor to pay the pre-petition claims of vendors which are critical for the continued operation of the debtor's business, often referred to as "critical vendors." This doctrine is referred to as the necessity doctrine and is grounded in sections 105(a) and 363(b) of the Bankruptcy Code.

There are a number of weaknesses in this theory. Only the debtor (not a creditor or an indenture trustee) has standing to seek approval of a payment under the necessity doctrine. Further, such approval is generally granted only when there is a serious risk that the creditor will stop providing services if the creditor is not paid. For that reason, many bankruptcy courts deny critical vendor status to any creditor under an executory contract.

In the case of an indenture trustee, there is no risk that the services will be discontinued if the trustee is not paid: even if the trustee resigns, it must continue to provide services until a successor is appointed. The indenture trustee is bound by a contract — the indenture — under which it has duties both to the obligor and the holders. For all of these reasons, the necessity doctrine is not usually an avenue for payment to an indenture trustee.

6. Bankruptcy Code § 506(b)

Section 506(b) provides that to the extent that an allowed secured claim is secured by property, the value of which is greater than the amount of the claim, the holder of the claim is entitled to recover reasonable fees, costs, and charges provided in the agreement under which the claim arises. This provision allows a fully secured creditor to recover its fees and expenses where those fees and expenses are provided for in its governing agreement (such as an indenture). Thus, a trustee under a secured indenture may recover its fees and expenses as part of its secured claim pursuant to section 506(b).

Section 506(b) applies only to fully secured claims. If the value of the collateral is less than the outstanding obligations under the indenture (in other words, if the claim is undersecured), section 506(b) does not apply.

PRACTICE TIP

In the case of a fully secured indenture, the trustee's fees and expenses should be included in the treatment provisions of a plan and paid as part of the treatment of the secured claims. If the plan provides for the secured claims to be exchanged for new securities, the plan should also provide that the indenture trustee's fees and expenses are to be paid in cash.

15.5 Why are indenture trustees' fees and expenses not automatically treated as administrative expenses under section 503 of the Bankruptcy Code?

Administrative expense treatment would appear to be the most logical and direct approach to the payment of an indenture trustee's fees and expenses in a chapter 11 bankruptcy case. Unfortunately, administrative expense treatment of trustees' fees and expenses has not been adopted by the majority of courts.

In a number of high profile cases, the United States Trustee has objected to plan terms providing for the payment of the indenture trustee's fees and expenses as administrative expenses on the grounds that bankruptcy law prohibits such treatment unless the indenture trustee is able to demonstrate that it made a "substantial contribution in the case" under section 503(b)(3)(D) of the Bankruptcy Code. United States Trustees have argued that section 503(b) of the Bankruptcy Code comprehensively governs payments to indenture trustees, Committee members, and their professionals in a bankruptcy case, and no administrative expense payments may be made unless expressly authorized by section 503(b).

In the case, *In re Lehman Brothers Holdings Inc.,* 487 B.R 181 (Bankr. S.D.N.Y. 2013), the United States Trustee objected to the payment, under the debtor's plan, of the fees and expenses of indenture trustees that served on the creditors' committee. The Court approved the plan, as well as the provisions for payment of the fees of committee members, including the indenture trustees. This was in accordance with *In re Adelphia Communications Corp.*, 441 B.R. 6, 14 (Bankr. S.D.N.Y. 2010). In *Adelphia*, the Court approved a plan in which the debtor provided for payment of such fees under the broad authority given a debtor under section 1123(b)(6). That section provides that "a plan 'may' 'include any other appropriate provision not inconsistent with the applicable provisions of this title.'"

In *Lehman*, Judge Peck wrote:

> [T]he Court rejects as overly restrictive the reading of Section 503(b) advanced by the [United States Trustee] in her objection to the requested fees. The [United States Trustee]'s argument is built on the proposition that Section 503(b) has a controlling and preclusive impact and is the exclusive pathway by which a member of an official committee can ever be entitled to receive compensation for legal fees incurred while serving on such a committee. . . .
>
> That reading goes too far and confuses the capacity to assert a substantial contribution claim with the ability to be granted the functional equivalent of such a right to payment under a plan that has been ratified so overwhelmingly by creditors. The flaw in the [United States Trustee]'s argument is the embedded assumption that the administrative claim formulation of Section 503(b) functions as a trump card that extends across the Bankruptcy Code to block the formulation of a plan that proposes independent grounds for granting comparable payment rights. There is no basis for such a contention.

Lehman, 487 B.R. at 185-86. The Court overruled the United States Trustee's objection, holding that the described plan provision "easily fits within the broad spectrum of section 1123(b)(6)." *Id.* at 191.

The United States Trustee appealed the bankruptcy court's decision in *Lehman*. On appeal, the District Court overturned the bankruptcy court's decision, holding that section 503(b) is the exclusive avenue for payment of administrative expenses and the section excludes Committee members' professional fees. *Davis v. Elliot Mgmt. Corp.* (*In re Lehman Bros. Holdings Inc.*), 508 B.R. at 289.

The District Court rejected the argument that a debtor may — under a plan, and pursuant to the broad authority granted by section 1123(b)(6) to include provisions in a plan that meet the needs of a particular case — propose to pay amounts that are not specifically defined as administrative expenses under section 503. The indenture trustees moved the District Court to certify an interlocutory appeal, but the motion was denied. *Davis v. Elliot Mgmt. Corp.* (*In re Lehman Bros. Holdings Inc.*), No. 13 Civ 2211 (RJS), 2014 WL 3408574, at *2 (S.D.N.Y. June 30, 2014).

15.6 Do indentures provide specifically for administrative expense treatment of the trustees' fees and expenses in a bankruptcy case?

Yes. Most indentures contain language along the lines of Model Indenture § 7.07, which provides in pertinent part:

> [W]hen the Trustee incurs expenses or renders services after an Event of Default [involving bankruptcy] occurs, the expenses and the compensation for the services are intended to constitute expenses of administration under any Bankruptcy Law.

Under the Bankruptcy Code, administrative expense allowances must be approved by the bankruptcy court and must meet the requirements set forth in section 503(b). While an applicable indenture provision may be useful to an indenture trustee in supporting its argument for payment, it is not, in itself, binding on a bankruptcy court or dispositive as to the requirements of section 503(b). In short, although the indenture provision is important and useful, it is not a guarantee of administrative expense treatment.

15.7 If the administrative expense provision in indentures is not enforceable as such, why have it?

While the provision is not binding in the sense that it does not obviate the application of the section 503 requirements or compel the bankruptcy court to grant administrative expense treatment, the provision is useful in supporting the trustee's claim. Specifically, it is evidence of the debtor's intent to treat the services of the indenture trustee as ongoing and necessary post petition services, and as such supports the trustee's claim for payment.

15.8 Can the indenture trustee claim administrative expense treatment based on the substantial contribution provisions of the Bankruptcy Code?

The substantial contribution sections of the Bankruptcy Code, sections 503(b)(3)(D), 503(b)(4), and/or 503(b)(5), have rarely been invoked successfully by an indenture trustee. Indeed, they are largely inapplicable to the services provided by an indenture trustee.

The term "substantial contribution" is not defined in the Bankruptcy Code. Under the relevant case law, in order to meet this standard a claimant must generally show that it took extraordinary actions that led to an actual and demonstrable (or direct and material) benefit to the debtor's estate.

There is a split of authority as to whether or not the claimant's intent to benefit the estate is relevant. *Compare Lebron v. Mechem Fin. Inc.*, 27 F.3d 937, 944 (3d Cir. 1994) (holding that intent is relevant), *and Haskins v. U.S. (In re Lister)*, 846 F.2d 55, 57 (10th Cir. 1988) (same), *with Speights & Runyan v. Celotex Corp. (In re Celotex Corp.)*, 227 F.3d 1336, 1339 (11th Cir. 2000) (holding that intent is not relevant), *and Hall Fin. Group, Inc. v. DP Partners Ltd. P'ship (Matter of DP Partners*

Ltd. P'ship.), 106 F.3d 667, 673 (5th Cir. 1997) (same). Several courts, including the bankruptcy courts in the District of Delaware and the Southern District of New York, have viewed the claimant's intent to benefit the estate as relevant, disallowing a substantial contribution claim where the claimant was merely pursuing its own interests. *See, e.g., In re Dana Corp.*, 390 B.R. 100, 108 (Bankr. S.D.N.Y. 2008); *In re Summit Metals, Inc.*, 379 B.R. 40, 51 (Bankr. D. Del. 2007), *aff'd*, 406 Fed. App'x 634 (3d Cir. 2011).

Because an indenture trustee's role is to advance the interests of its holders (not the debtor or other creditors), an indenture trustee's fees and expenses rarely qualify as substantial contribution claims. Claims for fees and expenses may meet the substantial contribution standard where an indenture trustee pursues a claim on behalf of the estate, although such circumstances are rare.

PRACTICE TIP

There may be "work-arounds" to avoid the imposition of the limitation imposed by the District Court's ruling in *Lehman*. Possible approaches which may avoid the *Lehman* limitation are:

- Incorporating a "substantial contribution" finding into the plan;
- Seeking approval of payment of the indenture trustee's fees and expenses as a settlement under Rule 9019 of the Federal Rules of Bankruptcy Procedure;
- Including payment of the indenture trustee's fees in a plan-support agreement negotiated between the debtor and holders, which is approved by the bankruptcy court prior to the confirmation hearing; or
- Including a cash amount sufficient to pay the indenture trustee's fees and expenses in the treatment of the holders' claims.

15.9 Can fees and expenses of the trustee under a subordinated notes indenture be paid, if distributions to holders are subject to the claims of senior holders?

Yes. Usually the fees and expenses of the trustee under a subordinated indenture are not subordinated. The Model Indenture provides:

> **Section 11.12. Trustee's Rights to Compensation, Reimbursement of Expenses and Indemnification.**
>
> The Trustee's rights to compensation, reimbursement of expenses and indemnification under sections 6.08 and 7.07 are not subordinated.

Model Indenture § 11.12. This provision was intended as a clarification of the trustee's rights to priority with respect to its fees, expenses, and indemnification claims under a subordinated notes indenture. Many indentures that do not contain this express language are nevertheless intended to exempt from subordination, the trustee's rights to compensation, expense reimbursement, and indemnification. The Model Indenture language states this directly, so as to avoid controversy concerning the effect of subordination on such rights.

The Model Indenture's waterfall provisions also reflect the intent that the indenture trustee's rights to compensation, expense reimbursement and indemnification are not subordinated to, and have priority over, the senior debt:

> **Section 6.08. Priorities.**
>
> After an Event of Default any money or other property distributable in respect of the Company's obligations under this Indenture shall be paid in the following order:

> First: to the Trustee (including any predecessor Trustee) for amounts due under Section 7.07;
>
> Second: to holders of Senior Debt to the extent required by Article 11[.]

Model Indenture § 6.08.

15.10 Given the lack of definitive, controlling case law holding that indenture trustees have a right to be paid as administrative expenses, how and why do fees get paid in so many cases?

First, indenture trustees add value in chapter 11 cases. Indenture trustees sit on Committees. They participate in plan negotiations. They facilitate communications between and among the holders, other creditor constituencies, and the debtor. They are often called upon to assist the debtor's noticing and solicitation agent in the solicitation, noticing and balloting processes. Indenture trustees are essential in the distribution process. Their expertise and services are especially important where the distribution takes the form of new securities.

Given the involvement of the indenture trustee in a case, and the usefulness of the indenture trustee to the debtor and the Committee, the indenture trustee is in a position to influence how its fees are treated in the process.

Second, when holders are actively negotiating with the debtor, they have leverage to insist that all of the "bond-side" fees are paid. This usually means not just the fees and expenses of the indenture trustees, but fees and expenses of counsel and advisors to major holders or groups of holders.

Third and perhaps most importantly, the Committee has real power in a plan negotiation. It is extraordinarily difficult to obtain confirmation of a plan without Committee support. This in itself gives a Committee — on which indenture trustees typically sit as members

— the leverage to insist that indenture trustees' fees and expenses be paid in the chapter 11 plan.

As a last resort, the indenture trustee may object to a plan that does not provide for payment of its fees and expenses, and/or seek an order directing payment from the bankruptcy court.

PART V

THE CHAPTER 11 PLAN AND DISCLOSURE STATEMENT

PART V:

The Chapter 11 Plan and Disclosure Statement

Chapter 16. The Chapter 11 Plan

16.1 What is a chapter 11 plan?

A chapter 11 plan is a global restructuring instrument which addresses all of a debtor's existing contractual and creditor relationships, and defines the terms of those relationships going forward. The plan is the legal vehicle by which the debt reorganization of a company is accomplished in a chapter 11 case. The intended objective of a chapter 11 case is the confirmation of a plan.

A plan may be proposed by the debtor, or, in rare instances, by creditors or other parties in interest, *see* 11 U.S.C. § 1112, and must be approved (or "confirmed") by the bankruptcy court in order to take effect. *See* 11 U.S.C. § 1129. The Bankruptcy Code sets out in detail what can and cannot be done in a plan, as well as the roadmap of requirements for a debtor in proposing a plan and seeking its approval by the court. 11 U.S.C. §§ 1122-1129.

16.2 What is the role of the indenture trustee in the formulation and negotiation of a plan?

While the indenture trustee is not entitled to vote or consent to a plan or bind the holders to any restructuring affecting their rights to principal and interest, the indenture trustee may negotiate with the debtor over the terms of a plan. In fact, the indenture trustee is typically involved in plan negotiations. While the indenture trustee cannot agree to a plan on behalf of holders, it can provide guidance on the terms of a plan to be proposed to holders. The indenture trustee can communicate to the debtor what holders want and the terms the holders would likely support.

16.3 Is it prudent for the indenture trustee to be involved in plan negotiations, given that it cannot vote or bind holders to a plan?

This is a question to be answered on a case-by-case basis, but generally the answer is yes. Plan negotiations often involve numerous parties and constituencies: the debtor, senior secured lenders, unsecured debt security holders (and sometimes multiple tranches), landlords, employee groups or unions, trade creditors, and tort claimants.

Plans are the product of hard-fought negotiations in which parties or groups that are unrepresented or underrepresented fare poorly, or at least not as well as constituencies that are vigorously represented.

Under the prudent person standard, it is incumbent on an indenture trustee to provide for adequate representation of holders' interests during a chapter 11 case (subject to the terms and conditions of the indenture), including the informal process during which a debtor will negotiate and formulate a plan. In most cases this means involvement in plan negotiations.

16.4 What are some of the circumstances that give rise to the indenture trustee's involvement in plan negotiations?

The indenture trustee's involvement in plan negotiations generally stems from one of the following situations:

(1) The holders are mainly retail holders who are unfamiliar with a bankruptcy process and are not in a

position to retain counsel individually to represent their interests, or do not have large enough holdings to have any influence in a plan negotiation. In the case of a largely retail holder body, the indenture trustee, pursuant to the prudent person standard, will represent the holders, who would otherwise be unrepresented in the process.

(2) The holders are sophisticated institutional holders who do not want to enter into a confidentiality agreement restricting their rights to buy and sell the securities. A debtor usually requires such an agreement as part of entering into negotiations with its creditors. In this situation, the indenture trustee may conduct negotiations, usually with holders' directional involvement and advice. At some point in the negotiations, economic decisions are necessary that require the holders to enter into a confidentiality agreement and become restricted in order to take a direct role in negotiations. The indenture trustee can inform holders when the discussions have reached a point when it may be appropriate for them to become restricted in order to participate in negotiations directly.

(3) The indenture trustee serves on a Committee, as the representative of the holders, and the Committee is engaged in negotiations with the debtor on behalf of the unsecured creditors collectively.

(4) A group of holders have entered into a confidentiality agreement with the debtor and are actively involved in negotiations with the debtor. In this scenario, the indenture trustee's involvement

facilitates the process and assists in implementation of the restructuring being negotiated between the holders and the debtor. The indenture trustee's involvement also provides assurance that the interests of the holders who are not directly involved are not prejudiced.

16.5 What is a rights offering?

A rights offering is an offer to the debtor's existing holders (and sometimes to other creditors or shareholders) to acquire shares in the reorganized company, in proportion to their holdings, for a discounted price relative to the value of the shares. Rights are sometimes transferable, allowing the holder to sell them on the open market. More typically, they are not transferable, or not transferable separately from the underlying debt security.

A rights offering is also a means for a debtor to raise cash to fund its emergence from chapter 11, in addition to any other exit financing. A plan may include a rights offering, although it will usually be negotiated and approved prior to confirmation as part of a plan support agreement.

16.6 Why is exit financing needed?

Debtors are required to pay all administrative expenses in full in order to emerge from chapter 11. These include all reorganization expenses (*e.g.*, professional fees) as well as the amounts needed to assume executory contracts and to repay outstanding debtor-in-possession financing. Most debtors do not have sufficient cash on hand to fund exit requirements as well as operating capital, and thus require exit financing.

16.7 What is a "back stop"?

In a rights offering, a "back stop" means a commitment by a creditor or creditors (such as a holder or group of holders) to buy any unsubscribed shares.

16.8 What is a "lock-up" agreement?

A "lock-up" refers to an agreement between a debtor and creditors and/or other parties in interest to support a plan proposal. When such an agreement is entered prior to the chapter 11 filing, it is often called a "restructuring support agreement" or "RSA." When entered during the chapter 11 case, it is usually called a "plan support agreement" or "PSA."

An RSA or PSA is subject to court approval and usually contains a number of conditions and protections which allow the parties to terminate the agreement under certain circumstances. One of these is the "fiduciary out," which refers to a provision which allows a debtor to pursue a different plan from the one agreed to if it is in the best interest of the estate to do so.

RSAs and PSAs usually contain milestones, *i.e.,* deadlines by which the debtor must take certain steps, such as filing a plan, or by which certain events must occur, such as obtaining approval of a disclosure statement, entry of a confirmation order, or the occurrence of an effective date. Where the PSA or RSA calls for a sale of the debtor's assets, the milestones will include dates by which steps in the sale process must be accomplished.

16.9 May the indenture trustee enter into or sign a restructuring or plan support agreement?

Generally speaking, the answer is no. An RSA or PSA is an agreement by supporting creditors to vote for a plan. The indenture trustee does not have the right to vote on a plan on behalf of holders or to bind the holders to a plan treatment, and these rights are expressly reserved to holders under most indentures. Thus, the indenture trustee's agreement to an RSA or PSA would appear to be beyond the trustee's powers under the indenture.

The RSA or PSA may provide that the indenture trustee, at the direction of majority holders, take or refrain from taking certain actions in furtherance of the plan supported by the holders signing the RSA or PSA. For example, the RSA or PSA may provide that the indenture trustee not object to the plan. Indenture trustees are sometimes asked to sign as an acknowledging party to RSA or PSA because of such provisions. While the decision whether to sign or not is a matter in the discretion of each indenture trustee in light of its own corporate trust policies, most indenture trustees decline to sign an RSA or PSA, even as an acknowledging party.

An RSA or PSA may also provide for the fees and expenses of the indenture trustee and the supporting holders to be paid, either upon approval of the PSA or RSA, or the confirmation of the plan.

16.10 What course of action should an indenture trustee take when the proposed plan being negotiated includes consideration that is not available to all holders?

In some cases, an issuer or a group of holders might present a proposal that includes aspects (such as rights offering or equity investment) which as a legal or practical matter is limited to certain investors, such as qualified institutional buyers or accredited investors.[8]

In such a situation, an indenture trustee may provide input into the process. It is generally the indenture trustee's position that a rights offering or other investment opportunity should be made available to all holders. The trustee may ask the debtor to provide cash or some other form of consideration in the plan for holders who cannot participate in a rights offering, or who do not wish to invest new money. This is not always feasible, and, in any event, is outside the indenture trustee's control: the indenture trustee is not directly a party to the rights offering and often has limited, if any, influence on its terms. Moreover, even when alternative consideration is provided, such consideration is usually not the economic equivalent of the rights offering. The reason for this is that holders who are willing and able to take the risk of investing new money may be in a position to extract additional value, while those who do not expend new money will generally not be.

While the indenture trustee should try to ensure fair and non-discriminatory treatment of all the holders, the debtor does not have to offer or accept a new money investment. The debtor, as a fiduciary, may limit the offering for any number of valid reasons, including the financial strength and reliability of investors. Moreover, rights offerings are inherently speculative and often difficult to value. It would be impossible as a practical matter for the indenture trustee to equalize investment opportunities made available to holders in a chapter 11 case, such as a rights offering or other debtor financing, and the indenture trustee is under no duty to do so.

Cash-exercise stock options or warrants offered as part of a plan treatment present similar considerations, in that they may not be available to be exercised by all holders, or even desirable to all holders. If practicable, the indenture trustee should seek to have the debtor provide for cashless exercise options in the plan or an alternative that is available to all holders.

16.11 Should the indenture trustee support or recommend a plan?

By and large, the answer is no. The indenture trustee's recommendation of a plan could be viewed as providing investment advice, which is outside of the indenture trustee's role and authority.

As to supporting a plan, this is a grey area. Some indenture trustees will not support a plan directly, because such support might be construed as recommending the plan to holders, which arguably might constitute investment advice. However, an indenture trustee may, in its capacity as a member of a Committee, agree to the Committee's support or recommendation of a plan.

16.12 Are there certain provisions in a plan that are necessary from an indenture trustee's perspective?

Ideally, a plan should include:

> (1) Provisions for payment of the indenture trustee's fees and expenses, including the fees and expenses of counsel and agents.
>
> (2) Distribution provisions that provide for the trustee to make distributions in a manner that is consistent with the indenture and with procedures of the trustee and DTC.
>
> (3) Discharge of the trustee and cancellation of the indenture, with a carve-out for certain rights of the trustee, including preservation of the trustee's charging lien.
>
> (4) Exculpation, and if legally available, releases of the indenture trustee in connection with its actions during the case and the formulation, approval, and implementation of the plan.

16.13 What provisions should be in a plan concerning the indenture trustee's fees and expenses?

There is no formula that fits every case. The most common approach is the inclusion of language in the "Implementation" or "Miscellaneous" section providing for payment of the fees and expenses of the indenture trustee on the effective date of the plan, without the need for separate bankruptcy court approval, subject to the indenture trustee providing reasonable documentation with an opportunity for the debtor, the Committee, and the United States Trustee to review and object on the grounds of reasonableness.

An alternative seen in some plans is the express inclusion of the indenture trustee's fees and expenses in the allowed administrative expense claims to be paid in full on the effective date of the plan. While the administrative expense approach is intellectually honest, this treatment has drawn objections in many cases and cannot currently be regarded as the best practice. As of the date of this writing, the allowance and treatment of indenture trustees' fees as an administrative expense claim is disfavored in light of the *Lehman* case, discussed in Chapter 15.

A third alternative is the inclusion of the payment of the indenture trustee's fees and expenses in the claim treatment section of the plan. Under this approach, the plan will provide for the payment of fees and expenses of the indenture trustee as part of the treatment of the class of claims of holders.

The first approach, the inclusion of a provision in the "Implementation" or "Miscellaneous" sections, accomplishes the same result as administrative expense treatment but draws fewer objections. Under the "implementation" or "miscellaneous" approach, the fees and expenses are not labeled as administrative expense claims, but the plan provides that the fees and expenses are paid in full, in cash, on the effective date of the plan, as a plan implementation matter — in essence, as a necessary expense of effectuating the plan, as opposed to an allowed administrative expense. Largely because of the controversy over whether indenture trustees' fees are allowable under the Bankruptcy Code as administrative expenses, inclusion in the "Implementation" or "Miscellaneous" provisions is a currently favored approach.

PRACTICE TIP

This is an example of plan language providing for the payment of the indenture trustee's fees and expenses:

> Notwithstanding any provision in the Plan to the contrary, the Debtor or Reorganized Debtor shall promptly pay in cash in full the reasonable and documented fees and expenses incurred by the Indenture Trustee without the filing of fee applications with or approval by the bankruptcy court; provided that each party and its counsel shall provide the Debtor and the Committee with invoices (or other documentation as the Debtor or Committee may reasonably request) for which it seeks payment within five days after the entry of the Confirmation Order, and provided that the Debtor and Committee have no objection to such fees, such fees shall be paid within five business days of the Effective Date. To the extent that the Debtor or Committee objects to any of the fees and expenses of the Indenture Trustee or its counsel or advisors, the Debtor shall not be required to pay any disputed portion of such fees until a resolution of such objection is agreed to by the Debtor, the Committee, and the Indenture Trustee, or a further order of the bankruptcy court upon a motion by the Indenture Trustee.

16.14 What provisions should be included regarding distribution mechanics?

First, the plan should state that distributions to holders should be made to the indenture trustee, as paying agent under the indenture, and that the indenture trustee shall make the distributions to holders in accordance with the terms of the indenture.

With respect to mechanics, there is no single formulation that fits the needs of every case and every indenture trustee. General language stating that distributions will be made in accordance with the standard procedures of DTC will give the indenture trustee the flexibility to work out the most suitable procedure with DTC. On the other hand, more specific language in the plan may tend to mitigate uncertainty when the indenture trustee instructs DTC with respect to a distribution.

16.15 What type of carve-outs are necessary to preserve the indenture trustee's rights?

Plans customarily contain provisions for automatic cancellation and discharge of all notes, instruments, and indentures under which the debtor is obligated. An indenture trustee should insist that the cancellation language contain a carve-out for its rights under the indenture to fees, expenses, and indemnification claims, including the preservation and exercise of its charging lien. The cancellation language should also expressly allow the indenture trustee to make distributions and to take any actions necessary after confirmation.

PRACTICE TIP

This is an example of an indenture cancellation provision in a plan. The italicized language illustrates carve-outs of the indenture trustee's rights:

> Cancellation of Notes, Instruments, and Interests. On the Effective Date, except as otherwise provided for in the Plan or any agreement, instrument or

other document incorporated in the Plan or the Plan Supplement, the Indenture and all other instruments or agreements evidencing any Claims or Interests (other than intercompany interests), shall be deemed automatically extinguished and cancelled with respect to the Debtor only, without any further act or action under any applicable agreement, law, regulation, order or rule, and the obligations of the Debtor under Indenture, and all other instruments evidencing any Claims or Interests shall be automatically discharged. The Holders of or parties to such cancelled notes and all other agreements and instruments shall have no rights against the Debtor arising from or relating to such notes, Indenture, and all other agreements and instruments or the cancellation thereof, except the rights provided pursuant to the Plan. *Notwithstanding the foregoing, and notwithstanding confirmation or consummation of this Plan, any such indenture or agreement that governs the rights of the Holder of a Claim shall continue in effect (and the Indenture Trustee shall remain as trustee, register and paying agent) for the purposes of: (1) allowing Holders to receive distributions under the Plan; and (2) allowing the Indenture Trustee to make the distributions in accordance with the Plan and the Indenture, as applicable; (3) preserving any rights of the Indenture Trustee to payment of fees, expenses, and indemnification obligations as against any money or property distributable to Holders under the relevant indenture, including any rights to priority of payment and/or to exercise charging liens; (4) to permit the Indenture Trustee to enforce any obligations owed to it under the Plan; (5) to permit the Indenture Trustee to appear in the case or any proceeding in the case in which it is or may become a party.*

16.16 Can a plan provide for distribution on account of debt securities to be made to a party other than the indenture trustee so as to circumvent the indenture trustee's charging lien?

Sometimes a debtor will attempt to avoid the indenture trustee's charging lien by changing the paying agent with respect to the plan distribution, or by providing that distributions be paid either to holders directly or to a disbursing agent other than the indenture trustee. Such an action is prohibited by most indentures.

If the indenture waterfall provision is drafted to include all funds allocable or distributable on account of the securities, the indenture trustee can assert its charging lien with respect to the distributions whether or not they are paid to the trustee.

A plan should provide that distributions on account of debt securities be paid to or at the instruction of the indenture trustee for distribution as provided in the indenture. If the indenture trustee is unable to convince the debtor to have the plan provide accordingly, the indenture trustee may need to file a formal objection to the plan.

16.17 Can an indenture trustee obtain a release under a confirmed plan for its role in the chapter 11 case as a member of a Committee?

Yes, but only to a limited extent. Exculpations of indenture trustees for their role on the Committee and during the pendency of the bankruptcy cases for actions, other than for willful misconduct or gross negligence, are customarily included in plans, and have been upheld by bankruptcy courts generally. *See, e.g., In re Washington Mutual, Inc.* 442 B.R. 314, 350 (Bankr. D. Del. 2011) (*citing In re PWS Holding Corp.*, 228 F.3d 224, 246 (3d Cir. 2000)).

While the debtor has broad latitude in granting releases on behalf of itself or its estate to parties under a plan, including the indenture trustee and Committee members, the ability to incorporate a broader release in a plan, releasing claims on behalf of other parties, is much more constrained. Federal courts are split on the threshold question of whether the bankruptcy court may approve the release of non-debtor parties in a confirmed chapter 11 plan. In the majority of circuits (the First, Second, Third, Fourth, Sixth, Seventh, Eleventh, and D.C. Circuits), such releases are permitted under certain circumstances. *SE Property Holdings, LLC v. Seaside Engineering & Surveying, Inc. (In re Seaside Engineering & Surveying, Inc.)*, No. 14-11590, J. Anderson, at p. 3 (11th Cir. Mar. 12, 2015), *In re Continental Airlines,* 203 F.3d 203, 212 (3d Cir. 2000); *Class Five Nev. Claimants v. Dow Corning Corp. (In re Dow Corning Corp.),* 280 F.3d 648, 657-58 (6th Cir. 2002); *In re Metromedia Fiber Network, Inc.,* 416 F.3d 136, 141 (2d Cir. 2005).

The ability of Committee members, including indenture trustees, to obtain third party releases for their service on the Committee has been greatly limited following the decision of the United States Bankruptcy Court for the District of Delaware in *Washington Mutual,* 442 B.R. at 350-51. While not binding on any other court, Judge Walrath's decision has been viewed as a bellwether decision in the area and represents the trend of well-reasoned authority.

Judge Walrath found that while Committee members, including indenture trustees, were appropriately given exculpation in the plan, the proposed third party releases (*i.e.,* the release of claims of creditors and parties in interest against the Committee members without the consent or agreement of the party to be bound by the release), did not meet the following well-established criteria necessary to sustain such releases:

> (1) An identity of interest between the debtor and the third party, such that a suit against the non-debtor will deplete assets of the estate;
>
> (2) Substantial contribution by the non-debtor to the plan;
>
> (3) The essentiality of the injunction to the reorganization to the extent that, without the injunction, there is little likelihood of success;
>
> (4) The overwhelming acceptance of the plan and release by a substantial majority of creditors; and
>
> (5) Payment of all or substantially all of the claims of the class or classes affected by the release.

Id., at 346. Judge Walrath rejected the notion that service on the Committee in itself constituted a substantial contribution to the reorganization. *Id.*, at 349-50.

The decision reflects the weight of reasoned authority in this area which requires that, in order to receive a broad release, the party receiving the release provide consideration in the form of money, property, or settlement of its claims.

In jurisdictions which recognize the bankruptcy court's authority to approve a release of a non-debtor effective against creditors or holders, the release must meet a multi-factor test. In some jurisdictions, there are additional factors beyond those recited in *Washington Mutual.*

Absent an identity of interest with the debtor, a cash or other tangible contribution to the plan, and/or an extraordinary service that would constitute a substantial contribution to the plan or the bankruptcy case, most bankruptcy courts will not approve a third-party release of an indenture trustee in a plan.

Chapter 17. Disclosure, Solicitation, and Voting

17.1 Who is entitled to vote on the plan with respect to claims arising under debt securities?

Under virtually all indentures, the right to vote on a chapter 11 plan is reserved to the security holders. For example, the Model Indenture provides:

> Nothing herein contained shall be deemed to authorize the Trustee … to authorize or consent to or accept or adopt on behalf of any Securityholder any plan of reorganization, arrangement, adjustment, or composition affecting the Securities or the rights of any Holder thereof, or to authorize the Trustee … to vote in respect of the claim of any Securityholder in any Proceeding.

Model Indenture, § 6.10.

Bankruptcy procedure mirrors these indenture provisions. Fed. R. Bankr. P. 3017(d) provides that a holder of a security of record on the date of the order approving the disclosure statement (or such other date fixed by the court after notice and a hearing) is a creditor for purposes of voting.

17.2 How do beneficial holders as a practical matter become informed of a plan and have the opportunity to vote, especially in light of the fact that their identities are not necessarily known by the indenture trustee or the debtor?

Fed. R. Bankr. P. 3017(e) requires the bankruptcy court to consider and determine the adequacy of the procedures to be used by the debtor in transmitting the plan, disclosure statement, and ballots to beneficial holders:

> (e) Transmission to beneficial holders of securities. At the hearing held pursuant to subdivision (a) of this rule, the court shall consider the procedures for transmitting the documents and information required by subdivision (d) of this rule to beneficial holders of stock, bonds, debentures, notes, and other securities, determine the adequacy of the procedures, and enter any orders the court deems appropriate.

Fed. R. Bankr. P. 3017(e).

17.3 How are the procedures for transmitting the solicitation materials to beneficial holders brought before the bankruptcy court for consideration?

In most chapter 11 cases, the debtor will file a motion to approve the disclosure statement, solicitation procedures, and form of ballots. The motion will seek approval of the form of solicitation package — the disclosure statement, plan, ballots, and any other materials the debtor intends to include in the package. Sometimes the solicitation package includes a recommendation of the debtor and/or the Committee to vote to accept the plan. The inclusion of these materials must also be approved by the bankruptcy court.

In cases where there are outstanding debt securities under an indenture, the motion should include proposed procedures for transmitting the solicitation package to the holders. The bankruptcy court evaluates these procedures to determine their adequacy under Fed. R. Bankr. P. 3017. The procedures will provide for the debtor (through its solicitation agent) to send the solicitation package directly to the DTC participants listed on the SPR, with instructions for them to retransmit promptly to their customers. The objective is to get the solicitation package into the hands of the beneficial holders in time for them to review it and vote, and then to return their ballots to the solicitation agent by the voting deadline.

The process can be uncertain and involve uncontrollable delays — it is indirect and depends on intermediaries. Therefore, building in sufficient time is necessary. Solicitation of debt securities generally requires a solicitation period of at least 45 days from the transmission of the solicitation package to the voting deadline.

17.4 What is the role of the indenture trustee in the disclosure statement approval, plan solicitation, and balloting process?

The indenture trustee should review the disclosure statement, plan solicitation materials, and voting procedures to identify any shortcomings that would affect the ability of the holders to consider the plan and cast a vote.

The trustee's examination should include the following:

- Are the claims of holders properly classified in accordance with section 1122 of the Bankruptcy Code?
- If the holders are impaired, are they being given the right to vote?
- Is the treatment of the debt securities clearly described, so that holders can understand what they will receive if the plan is confirmed?
- Are the proposed solicitation procedures sufficiently well designed to ensure that the beneficial holders will receive the plan and disclosure statement with sufficient time to review, make a decision, and vote before the deadline?
- Are the ballots clear? Are they written in a way that someone unfamiliar with a bankruptcy case would understand?

- If the plan includes a release by holders of claims against non-debtors, is the release clearly disclosed and are the holders provided the opportunity to reject or object to the release?
- Is the record date consistent with Fed. R. Bankr. P. 3017(d)? If a different date is proposed, is the date reasonable?
- Are the procedures for transmission of the solicitation package to beneficial holders and return of ballots to the balloting agent adequate?

PRACTICE TIP

The indenture trustee should identify any changes needed in the solicitation procedure and disclosure statement and attempt to have revisions made before the deadline to object to the motion to approve the disclosure statement. If all deficiencies are not addressed by the debtor prior to the time within which objections need to be filed, the indenture trustee should file an objection to the motion and seek to have the bankruptcy court rule on the issue.

17.5 What is the voting record date?

The voting record date is the date that determines eligibility of debt securities holders to vote on the plan. Holders of record on the voting record date are eligible to vote.

Fed. R. Bankr. P. 3017(d) provides that:

> . . . a form of ballot . . . shall be mailed to creditors . . . entitled to vote on the plan. . . . shall include holders of . . . bonds, debentures, notes and other securities of record on the date the order approving the disclosure statement is entered or another date fixed by the court, for cause, after notice and hearing.

PRACTICE TIP

The voting record date should generally be the date the disclosure statement is approved, which is the date expected in the distressed investing market. Variance from that date can cause confusion in the solicitation and voting process.

17.6 What amount of time is needed between the transmission of the solicitation package and the voting deadline, so that holders have sufficient time to vote?

While this varies case by case, depending largely on the number and composition of the beneficial holders body, 45 days is generally considered a minimum. On average, solicitation periods in cases involving debt securities range from 45 to 60 days. Solicitation periods are rarely less than 30 days and rarely over 90 days.

Chapter 18. Plan Confirmation, Effective Date, and Distribution

18.1 What is the indenture trustee's role after plan confirmation?

In most chapter 11 cases, the indenture is cancelled on the effective date, with rights remaining only to the extent specifically reserved in the plan. *See* 11 U.S.C. § 1123(a)(5)(F). In rare instances, a plan will not cancel the indenture but will cure defaults and reinstate the indenture under 11 U.S.C. § 1124(2).

In either instance, the indenture trustee no longer has a contractual duty after the effective date to act as a prudent person. The reason is that indenture defaults no longer exist, either because the indenture has been cancelled or the defaults have been cured. In either case, the prudent person standard no longer applies.

Where the indenture has been cancelled under the plan, the trustee may continue to have specific rights, duties, and powers as provided in the indenture to the extent such rights, duties and powers are preserved under the plan. The indenture trustee's primary role where the indenture has been cancelled is to serve as paying agent with respect to plan distributions. The indenture trustee prepares instructions to DTC for allocating plan distributions, and transmits the distributions to DTC for allocation to its participants' accounts.

PRACTICE TIP

Although they are not required by the indenture to do so, trustees typically provide notice to holders of the plan approval, the occurrence of the effective date, and distributions including final distribution.

A notice of final distribution will usually state that there will be no more distributions or notices from the indenture trustee.

18.2 Other than its role as a paying agent in connection with plan distributions, what roles might an indenture trustee be required to serve after the effective date?

Occasionally, the indenture trustee is a party to litigation after the effective date, such as when disputes over the indenture trustee's claim (or aspects of it) are not resolved before plan confirmation. This is unusual, as disputes concerning the claims of the holders and the indenture trustee are ordinarily resolved prior to the confirmation.

Debt securities are often the largest or among the largest claims in the case, and the approval of a requisite number of holders is generally necessary for a plan to be confirmed. The need to reach agreement with holders in order to obtain plan confirmation compels a debtor to resolve all disputes and reach an agreement over the treatment of the debt securities.

This is not always the case, of course. Where litigation or contested matters involving the indenture trustee are expected to be commenced or to continue after the effective date, the plan should expressly provide that, notwithstanding the cancellation of the indenture, the trustee retains the right to appear in any proceeding in which it is or may become a party.

18.3 May an indenture trustee serve on a post-confirmation committee or oversight board?

Members of the Committee may be selected to serve on a post-confirmation committee or an advisory board created to oversee the implementation of the plan or to supervise entities established under a plan to monetize assets or prosecute litigation claims for the benefit of creditors. Such entities can take the form of a creditors' trust, a litigation trust, a liquidation trust, or a plan administrator.

An indenture trustee may, but is not required to, serve on a post-confirmation or advisory board.

18.4 How can the indenture trustee pay for its fees and expenses incurred after confirmation?

Post confirmation fees and expenses are generally handled in one of three ways:

> (1) Under some plans, the payment of ongoing fees and expenses is expressly provided in the plan, and the reorganized debtor agrees to pay such expenses. This may occur where the reorganized debtor has agreed to compensate the indenture trustee for effectuating distributions made under the plan to holders, or to compensate the members of a post-confirmation committee or an oversight board on which the indenture trustee is appointed to serve.
>
> (2) In plans that do not provide for payment of post petition fees and expenses of the indenture trustee and that completely discharge the debtor from its obligations under the indenture, the indenture trustee can establish a reserve from distributions made under the plan. The reserve would be established through the indenture trustee's exercise of its charging lien or default waterfall rights, to the extent that those rights have been preserved under the plan.
>
> (3) Where litigation is being brought or defended at the request of holders, the indenture trustee can request that the holders pay the fees and expenses of the litigation.

PART VI

LITIGATION AND THE INDENTURE TRUSTEE

PART VI:

Litigation and the Indenture Trustee

Chapter 19. The Indenture Trustee's Right to Bring Actions

19.1 Does the indenture trustee have the right to bring actions?

Yes, the indenture trustee has the right to bring actions. The nature and scope of the actions which the indenture trustee may bring depend on the indenture.

With respect to TIA-qualified indentures, the indenture trustee has authority under section 317(a) of the TIA to sue to collect principal and interest, and, in a bankruptcy, to file any papers necessary or advisable to have claims under the indenture allowed in a bankruptcy case.

Section 317(a) of the TIA states as follows:

The indenture trustee shall be authorized:

> (1) In the case of a default in payment of the principal of any indenture security, when and as the same shall become due and payable, and in the case of default in the payment of the interest of any such security, when and as the same shall become due and payable and the continuance of such default for such period as may be prescribed in such indenture, to recover judgment in its own name and as trustee of an express trust, against the obligor upon the indenture securities for the

> whole amount of said principal and interest remaining unpaid; and
>
> (2) To file such proofs of claim and other papers or documents as may be necessary or advisable in order to have the claims of such trustee and of the indenture security holders allowed in any judicial proceedings relative to the obligor upon the indenture securities, its creditors, or its property[.]

TIA § 317(a)(1)-(2).

Section 317(a)(1) confers the right to bring suit to recover principal or interest after a default. Section 317(a)(2) appears to broaden this right by authorizing the indenture trustee, in a bankruptcy of the issuer, to file "claims of such trustee and of the indenture security holders .... relative to the obligor upon the indenture securities ...."

Most indentures, whether or not-TIA qualified, provide that the trustee has standing to bring suit to collect principal or interest, as well as to enforce any provision of the indenture or the securities. The authorization is typically contained in the remedies provisions in the default article of the indenture. An example is section 6.03 of the Model Indenture, which provides:

> **Section 6.03. Other Remedies.**
>
> If an Event of Default occurs and is continuing, the Trustee may pursue any available remedy to collect the payment of Principal or interest on the Securities or to enforce the performance of any provision of the Securities or this Indenture.

The remedies language in the Model Indenture is intended to include all actions, suits, or proceedings at law or equity arising under the indenture or the securities but does not encompass individual fraud claims of buyers or sellers of the securities under state or federal securities laws. *See Central Bank of Denver N.A. v. Deloitte & Touche*, 928 P.2d 754, 757-58 (Colo. Ct. App. 1996); Notes on the Revised Model Simplified Indenture.

Despite the Notes, the interpretation of the "Other Remedies" sections in indentures modeled after section 6.03 and the scope of actions that the trustee has authority to bring under such provisions has not been entirely clear. The question of whether the trustee may bring only contractual claims under the indenture or whether its authority includes non-contractual claims (such as common law and statutory claims) has been the subject of some controversy. While the Model Indenture language appears to encompass both contractual and non-contractual claims, there is no universally held view among the courts as to the scope of non-contractual claims that can be brought. *Compare LaSalle Nat'l Bank v. Perelman*, 141 F. Supp. 2d 451, 459-60 (D. Del. 2001) (a provision barring recourse "under the Securities" against any insider did not bar non-contractual claims for unjust enrichment or breach of fiduciary duty by the indenture trustee against insiders) *with Nationsbank, N.A. v. McGraw-Hill Cos.*, Civil Action No. H-94-0882, 1996 U.S. Dist. LEXIS 22414, at *18-20 (S.D. Tex. Dec. 12, 1996) (an indenture provision allowing the trustee to sue "under this Indenture" or "under any of the Bonds" allows the trustee to bring only contractual claims, and not tort claims).

A closely related question is the scope of actions that are covered by the so-called "no-action" clause in the indenture, discussed in the next chapter. The no-action clause precludes holders from filing certain actions unless such holders have first exhausted a number of requirements, including requesting that the trustee file the action.

PRACTICE TIP

The determination of whether an action can be brought by the indenture trustee is not always clearcut. The question may turn on some of these factors:

1. Whether the claims are contractual or non-contractual.

Contractual claims are claims arising under the indenture, such as recovery of principal or interest or for breach of an indenture covenant. The indenture trustee indisputably has standing after a default occurs to bring claims for principal and interest, or for breach of the indenture. Individual holders may also sue for their principal and interest due.

Non-contractual claims are those arising under common law or statutes. Whether the indenture trustee has the right to bring non-contractual claims will depend on whether the remedies provisions in the indenture can be read to include such claims, and whether the non-contractual claims are in fact brought to recover remedies that would ordinarily be considered contractual (for example, the recovery of principal and/or interest owed under the indenture).

2. Whether the indenture trustee is in privity with the defendant.

One consideration is whether the claims are against the issuer or against third parties who are not parties to the indenture, and thus not in privity with the trustee. Some courts concluded that the trustee has the right to bring an action only against those who are parties to the indenture or are bound by the indenture. This limitation may, for example, prevent a trustee from being able to bring a fraudulent conveyance claim against a transferee of an asset from the debtor, since the transferee is not a party to the indenture.

3. Whether the claims arise from the securities or from the purchase of the securities.

Another consideration is whether the claims arise out of the purchase of the securities (such as securities fraud claims) as opposed to the securities themselves. The weight of authority suggests that securities fraud claims may only be brought by holders, not by the indenture trustee, as these claims do not arise from the indenture or securities but arise from the purchase of the securities and are rights that may not be held by all holders. *See Regions Bank v. Blount Parrish & Co., Inc.*, No. 01CV0031, 2001 WL 726989, at *5 (N.D. Ill., June 27, 2001).

4. The operative language in the indenture.

The pertinent language is often found in the "Other Remedies" and "Limitation of Suits" provisions of the indenture corresponding to sections 6.03 and 6.06, respectively, of the Model Indenture. Language encompassing all rights, legal and equitable, whether arising under the indenture or the securities or under applicable law, may be interpreted more broadly than language simply referencing enforcement of rights arising under the indenture.

5. The no-action clause.

The language of the two provisions — the remedies provision and the limitation of suits (the "no-action") provision — should be comprehensive. If holders are prevented from bringing an action under the no-action provision, the indenture trustee should be empowered to bring the action under the remedies provisions. If there is a gap — an action which the holders are prevented from bringing themselves, but which the indenture trustee cannot bring on their behalf — some courts will construe the language in a manner that does not eliminate the rights to bring the action entirely. Under this view, the indenture is read so as to confer the right to bring the action on one of the parties (either the trustee or the holders, depending on the language of the indenture and the facts of the case).

19.2 How have the courts determined whether the indenture trustee has the right to bring a particular action?

The issue generally comes before a court after a suit is filed by the indenture trustee, and the defendant files a dispositive motion (a motion to dismiss the complaint or motion for summary judgment) challenging the trustee's right to bring the suit. The language of the indenture is almost always the starting point in judicial analysis and will often be relied upon by the court in determining the scope of the trustee's standing to bring the particular action.

In *Cortlandt St. Recovery Corp. v Hellas Telecomms., S.a.r.l.*, 47 Misc. 3d 544, 996 N.Y.S.2d 476 (Sup. Ct. N.Y. Cnty 2014), the indenture was virtually identical to section 6.03 of the Model Indenture. *See Cortlandt,* 47 Misc. d at 567, 996 N.Y.S.2d at 494. The *Cortlandt* court held that this language did not authorize the trustee to bring a fraudulent conveyance action, citing *Regions Bank*, 2001 WL 726989, at *5.

In *Regions Bank*, heavily relied upon in *Cortlandt,* the court held that '"any available remedy"' '"refers only to actions designed to collect the principal of, premium, if any, or interest on the Bonds or to enforce the performance of any provision of the bonds or the Indenture . . . [and] does not give [the trustee] power to protect any and all rights of the bondholders. . . .'" *Id,* and thus does not include fraud claims. The *Cortlandt* court similarly determined that because fraudulent conveyance claims were not claims brought on the notes but were tort claims against third parties, they were outside the scope of the trustee's authorization under the indenture.

The *Cortlandt* court noted that other courts have held, to the contrary, the trustee had authority to bring securities fraud claims when the indenture authorized the trustee to institute suits '"to protect and enforce its rights and the rights of the holders of the Bonds . . . in the enforcement of any other legal or equitable right as [the trustee], being advised by counsel, shall deem most effectual. . ..'" *See id* 47 Misc. 3d at 568, 996 N.Y.S.2d at 495, citing *In re Washington Pub. Power Supply Sys. Sec. Litig.,* 623 F. Supp. 1466, 1483 (D Wash. 1985), *aff'd,* 823 F.2d 1349 (9th Cir 1987).

The Delaware Chancery Court in *U.S. Bank Nat'l Ass'n v. U.S. Timberlands Klamath Falls, L.L.C.,* No. Civ.A. 112-N, 2004 WL 1699057, at *4 (Del.Ch. July 29, 2004) distinguished *Regions Bank* on the basis that the no-action clause in *Regions Bank* referred only to claims with respect to the indenture and did not limit the holders from bringing non-contractual claims. In contrast, in *U.S. Bank,* the limitations on the holders' filing suit applied both to contract claims (*e.g.*, claims arising under the indenture), and to non-contractual claims including statutory, tort, or common law claims (*e.g.*, claims arising with respect to the securities). Since the no-action clause required the holders to first request that the trustee bring non-contractual claims, it stands to reason that the indenture trustee had the right to bring them. *Id.* at *5.

The language of both the remedies clause and no-action clause is key. The case law is not entirely consistent, at least in part because the indenture language being construed has not been uniform.

19.3 Can the indenture trustee bring suit in its individual capacity or only in its representative capacity?

The indenture trustee has standing in a representative capacity only. In other words, the indenture trustee brings an action not in its individual capacity but solely as trustee under the indenture.

19.4 Can actions be brought against the indenture trustee in a representative capacity?

Yes. Actions are often filed against the indenture trustee in its representative capacity under the indenture. For example, issuers sometimes file declaratory judgment actions against the trustee seeking a determination that certain claims are not owed, such as make-whole premiums or post petition interest. *See, e.g., Chesapeake Energy Corp. v. Bank of N.Y. Mellon Trust Co., N.A.*, 773 F.3d 110, 113 (2d Cir. 2014) (issuer seeking declaratory ruling that its redemption notice to indenture trustee was timely and thus no make-whole was due under indenture).

PRACTICE TIP

Counsel to the indenture trustee should not accept service of a complaint without express authorization from the indenture trustee or without reviewing the complaint. If the complaint improperly names the trustee individually in the caption instead of naming the trustee solely in its representative capacity as trustee under the indenture, counsel should request that the caption and complaint be corrected before counsel accepts service.

19.5 Is an issuer or indenture trustee entitled to a jury trial in litigation involving the indenture?

Most indentures contain express waivers of the right to a jury trial. An example of a jury trial waiver in an indenture is the following:

> EACH OF THE COMPANY AND THE TRUSTEE, AND EACH HOLDER OF A NOTE BY ITS ACCEPTANCE THEREOF, HEREBY IRREVOCABLY WAIVES, TO THE FULLEST EXTENT PERMITTED BY APPLICABLE LAW, ANY AND ALL RIGHT TO TRIAL BY JURY IN ANY LEGAL PROCEEDING ARISING OUT OF OR RELATING TO THIS INDENTURE, THE NOTES OR THE TRANSACTION CONTEMPLATED HEREBY.

A jury trial waiver has a number of benefits to the indenture trustee. Jury trials are expensive and time consuming, and juries are unpredictable.

When litigation involving an indenture trustee ensues in bankruptcy court, a jury trial is usually not available, regardless of whether there is a jury trial waiver in the indenture. There is no right to a jury trial in most bankruptcy proceedings, as the bankruptcy court is a court of equity. According to the weight of authority, the debtor (*e.g.*, the issuer) is deemed to have waived its right to a jury trial by filing for bankruptcy, an equitable remedy. *See, e.g., N.I.S. Corp. v. Hallahan (Matter of Hallahan)*, 936 F.2d 1496, 1505 (7th Cir. 1991).

19.6 What type of actions do indenture trustees become parties to in a bankruptcy case?

Some common types of bankruptcy litigation to which indenture trustees are parties are actions brought by:

- the indenture trustee against the debtor seeking allowance of a make-whole premium
- a subordinated notes indenture trustee against a senior notes indenture trustee seeking a determination of entitlement under an "X-Clause" (exception to subordination) to new securities issued under a plan
- a debtor or Committee against the indenture trustee to invalidate a security interest under an indenture under the strong arm powers of the Bankruptcy Code (11 U.S.C. § 544)
- a debtor or liquidating trustee against the indenture trustee to avoid note redemption or note purchase transactions as constructive fraudulent transfers (11 U.S.C. § 548)[9]
- a debtor or Committee against the indenture trustee to invalidate a subsidiary guarantee as a constructive fraudulent transfer (11 U.S.C. § 548 and/or 544)
- a first lien indenture trustee against a second lien indenture trustee to enforce the terms of an intercreditor agreement
- a debtor against an indenture trustee to enjoin the trustee from suing a non-debtor

PRACTICE TIP

The indenture trustee may establish a website (typically via an extranet on its counsel's website) with material information concerning the chapter 11 case, and particularly, any disputes or litigation concerning the securities.

Chapter 20. Limitation on Suits (the "No Action" Clause)

20.1 Can holders sue an obligor directly?

Holders' rights to sue an obligor directly are limited by the so-called "no-action" clause, a common provision of indentures which imposes limitations and conditions upon holders' rights to take action against the obligor. No-action clauses serve to limit suits by individual holders by imposing preconditions on their right to file suit including a requirement to channel the claim through the indenture trustee.

Holders are precluded from pursuing remedies unless they collectively hold a threshold percentage of the debt securities (typically 25%) and request the indenture trustee to take the specified action. If the indenture trustee does not act upon the request within the time specified in the indenture, the holders may file the action.

A typical formulation of the no-action clause is in the Model Indenture:

> **Section 6.06. Limitation on Suits.**
>
> A Securityholder may pursue a remedy with respect to this Indenture or the Securities only if:
>
> (1) the Holder gives to the Trustee notice of a continuing Event of Default;
>
> (2) the Holders of at least 25% in Principal amount of the Securities make a request to the Trustee to pursue the remedy;

> (3) the Trustee either (i) gives to such Holders notice it will not comply with the request, or (ii) does not comply with the request within [15-30] days after receipt of the request; and
>
> (4) the Holders of a majority in Principal amount of the Securities do not give the Trustee a direction inconsistent with the request prior to the earlier of the date, if ever, on which the Trustee delivers a notice under Section 6.06(3)(i) or the expiration of the period described in Section 6.06(3)(ii).
>
> A Securityholder may not use this Indenture to prejudice the rights of another Securityholder or to obtain a preference or priority over another Securityholder.

Most indentures contain variations from Model Indenture language. One variation includes the requirement that holders provide an indemnification satisfactory to the indenture trustee as a condition of requesting the trustee to bring suit, a requirement absent from Model Indenture § 6.06. The rationale for omitting this limitation in the no-action clause is that the trustee has the right to indemnification under other sections of an indenture, will require satisfactory indemnification with respect to any action requested by holders, and can decline to file the action if it is not provided, clearing the way for holders to commence the suit themselves. The inclusion of an indemnification requirement in the no-action provision simply imposes an additional requirement which might block the holders' ability to take action if the trustee does not. The omission of an indemnification requirement from the no-action section does not eliminate the indenture trustee's right to indemnification, but its inclusion simply creates an unnecessary threshold before holders can commence an action.

Another common variation is the length of time within which the indenture trustee must respond to the holders' request to pursue a remedy. The commentary to the Model Indenture notes that the time periods of older indentures are simply too long given the speed of the modern bankruptcy process. While the Model Indenture proposes a period of 15-30 days, it is not unusual to see longer periods (such as 60 days) in an indenture.

Another important variation is the kinds of actions covered by the no-action clause.

20.2 What kinds of actions are subject to no-action provisions?

The answer to this question largely depends on the specific language of the indenture in question.

A key point is whether the no-action provision in question is broad — whether it includes, for example, actions "with respect to this Indenture or the Securities" — or narrow, in the sense that it would include actions "to enforce the Securities or the Indenture," as in the Model Indenture. The latter formulation arguably only encompasses contract and non-contract claims which seek to recover principal and interest or enforce rights arising under the indenture. On the other hand, the language "with respect to the Securities" would appear to encompass all rights arising in connection with the securities.

Further, if the no-action clause refers only to "the Indenture" and not to "the Securities," it is more likely to be construed narrowly to apply only to contract claims (*e.g.*, claims arising under the indenture), but not to statutory, tort, or common law claims (*e.g.*, claims arising with respect to the securities). As a result, if the language in the no-action clause refers only to claims under the indenture, individual holders may file actions asserting claims such as breach of fiduciary duty, fraudulent conveyance, fraud, and RICO, without the limitations and process of the no-action provisions. On the other hand, if the language refers to the securities, then holders most likely will not be able to maintain statutory, common law, or tort claims unless they follow the requirements of the no-action clause. *See Quadrant Structured Prods. Co., Ltd. v. Vertin*, 23 N.Y.3d 549, 560, 992 N.Y.S.2d 687, 694 (2014).

No-action clauses have generally been strictly construed. *See, e.g.*, *Cruden v. Bank of N.Y.*, 957 F.2d 961,968 (2d Cir. 1992); *RBC Capital Markets, LLC v. Education Loan Trust IV*, Civ. Action No. 6297-CS, 2011 WL 6152282, at *5 (Del. Ch. Dec. 6, 2011); *Akanthos Capital Mgmt., LLC v. CompuCredit Holdings Corp.*, 677 F.3d 1286, 1295-96 (11th Cir. 2012); *Quadrant Structured*, 23 N.Y.3d at 560, 992 N.Y.S.2d at 694. In *Akanthos*, the Eleventh Circuit held that a no-action clause applied to state law fraudulent conveyance claims against directors and officers, who were not parties to the indenture, because the no-action clause was premised on the nature of the claim, not the identity of the defendant.

Securities fraud claims are almost always considered to be outside the no-action clause limitations, regardless of whether the language is broad or narrow. *See In re Enron Corp. Sec., Derivative & "ERISA" Litig.*, No. MDL – 1446, Civ. Action Nos. H-01-3624, 03-5808, 2008 WL 744823, at *9 (S.D. Tex. Mar. 19, 2008), *McMahan & Co. v. Wherehouse Entm't, Inc.*, 859 F. Supp. 743, 748-49 (S.D.N.Y. 1994), *aff'd in part, rev'd in part*, 65 F.3d 1044 (2d Cir. 1995), *Victor v. Riklis*, No. 91 Civ. 2897(LJF), 1992 WL 122911, at *6 (S.D.N.Y. May 15, 1992); *Kusner v. First Pennsylvania Corp.*, 531 F.2d 1234, 1239 (3d Cir. 1976).

20.3 What is the effect of the no-action clause on the holders' rights to sue under TIA § 316(b)?

The no-action clause must be read with other provisions of the indenture, including a provision often referred to as the "anti-impairment" clause, a provision required by the TIA. *See* TIA § 316(b).

The exclusion of actions to enforce payment of principal and interest — rights which holders are expressly allowed by TIA § 316(b) — is central to the interpretation of the no-action provision.

The Model Indenture's formulation of the anti-impairment clause is as follows:

> **Section 6.07. Rights of Holders to Receive Payment.**
>
> Notwithstanding any other provision of this Indenture, the right of any Holder of a Security to receive payment of Principal and interest on the Security, on or after the respective due dates expressed in the Security, or to bring suit for the enforcement of any such payment on or after such respective dates, shall not be impaired or affected without the consent of the Holder.

Suits to collect principal and interest are expressly exempt from no-action clauses, *i.e.*, a holder need not comply with the requirements of the no-action clause prior to bringing a suit. *Cruden,* 957 F.2d at 968.

20.4 Are involuntary bankruptcy petitions subject to the no-action clause?

The weight of well reasoned authority has held that no-action clauses do not apply to the filing of or joining in an involuntary petition and that holders are not required to follow, and are not limited by, the no-action clause in filing an involuntary petition. *See, e.g., In re Envirodyne Indus., Inc.,* 174 B.R. 986, 997 (Bankr. N.D. Ill. 1994). In *Envirodyne*, the court stated that an involuntary petition seeks to obtain payment of principal and interest and therefore is an exception to the no-action clause.

20.5 Do beneficial holders have the right to request that the trustee bring suit under the no-action clause?

At least one court has held that only registered holders have rights under the no-action clause. *Cortlandt*, 47 Misc. 3d at 570, 996 N.Y.S.2d at 496-97. While the question is still unsettled, the preferred approach for beneficial holders seeking to file suit is to have the securities registered in their own name.

Chapter 21. Make-Whole Litigation

21.1 What is a make-whole provision?

A make-whole provision is a term in an indenture which protects holders' expectation of receiving their contractual interest over the term of the securities and compensates them for the loss of interest payments due to an early repayment of the securities. This is sometimes referred to as call protection. The other form of call protection is a "no-call" provision, an indenture provision prohibiting prepayment or early redemption of the securities.

A make-whole provision permits a redemption or prepayment before the maturity date, but only under certain conditions and/or only during certain time frames. One of the conditions is the payment of a premium in an amount calculated according to a formula in the indenture. The premium is designed to compensate the holders for the loss of the expected stream of contract-rate interest payments, assuming that the funds are reinvested under current market conditions.

In a climate of low interest rates, the interest rate for new financing may be less expensive than the interest rate for the existing debt securities. This creates an economic incentive for an issuer to redeem or refinance debt securities. The imposition of a make-whole premium, however, would eliminate the economic benefit of refinancing. Thus, an issuer may use chapter 11 to attempt to avoid the payment of a make-whole premium, in order to realize the economic benefit of refinancing.

21.2 Does the issuer's filing of a chapter 11 case eliminate the holders' entitlement to a make-whole claim?

The issue has not been entirely settled. Most of the courts which have considered make-whole claims have disallowed them, although the reasons are not uniform. Make-whole claims have been allowed in limited factual circumstances, such as those involving a solvent debtor. The case law reflects several analytical approaches, but is not uniform or clearcut.

21.3 In what context do make-whole disputes typically arise?

Make-whole disputes generally arise in cases in which the principal and interest obligations under the indenture will be fully paid, and estate funds, if not applied to the make-whole claim, would be potentially available for junior creditors or equity. In this situation, holders who assert the make-whole premium, on one hand, and junior creditors or equity holders, on the other hand, are competing for entitlement to the available funds. This dynamic creates pressure on the debtor to challenge the make-whole premium, so that the available funds can be allocated to other creditors.

The circumstance in which a claim for a make-whole premium is asserted is usually when the debtor proposes to pay the holders' claims in cash pursuant to a chapter 11 plan. Rarely, a debtor may seek to repay the holders' claims, in whole or in part, outside a plan, using funds on hand or a debtor-in-possession financing.[10] This might occur in a solvent estate where post petition interest is accruing at a rate higher than the debtor's current cost of funds.

Another context in which a make-whole claim will be asserted is a debt-for-debt or debt-for-equity exchange in a plan. In other words, the debtor proposes to treat the debt securities claims under a plan by issuing and distributing new debt securities with more issuer-favorable terms, or equity securities in the reorganized debtor. Under most indentures, it is less clear whether such treatment triggers the obligation to pay a make-whole premium. Nevertheless, make-whole claims are often asserted in this context as well.

21.4 Does a bankruptcy filing automatically accelerate the outstanding amounts due under the indenture?

Several courts have held that bankruptcy automatically accelerates principal amounts owed by the debtor, relying on section 101 (5) (A) of the Bankruptcy Code. *U.S. Trust Co. of N.Y. v. LTV Steel Co. (In re Chateaugay Corp.)*, 150 B.R. 529, 542 (Bankr. S.D.N.Y. 1993), ("[Debtor's] Chapter 11 filing automatically, by operation of bankruptcy law, accelerated the entire principal amount of each Series of Bonds. . . . "), *aff'd*, 170 B.R. 551 (S.D.N.Y. 1994); *In re Manville Forest Prods. Corp.*, 43 B.R 293, 297 (Bankr. S.D.N.Y. 1984) ("It is a basic tenet of the Bankruptcy Code that [b]ankruptcy operates as the acceleration of the principal amount of all claims against the debtor.") (internal quotation marks omitted), *aff'd in part, rev'd in part*, 60 B.R. 403 (S.D.N.Y. 1986). *See also In re AMR Corp.*, 485 B.R. 279, 290 n.7 (Bankr. S.D.N.Y.), *aff'd*, 730 F.3d 88 (2d Cir. 2013); *cert. denied*, 134 S. Ct. 1888 (2014); *In re Solutia Inc.*, 379 B.R. 473, 484-85 (Bankr. S.D.N.Y. 2007); (relying on 11 U.S.C. § 502).

Some indentures contain language specifying that upon an event of default due to a bankruptcy filing, the full principal amount outstanding under the indenture is immediately due and payable. It has been argued that such an automatic acceleration clause is an unenforceable *ipso facto* clause under section 365 (e)(1). Courts are split on this question. *Compare In re W.R. Grace & Co.,* 475 B.R. 34, 153-54 (D. Del. 2012), *aff'd*, 729 F.3d 332 (3d Cir. 2013) (holding that the *ipso facto* clause unenforceable under bankruptcy law), *with In re AMR Corp.*, 730 F.3d 88, 106-07 (2d Cir. 2013 (holding that the

Bankruptcy Code does not categorically prohibit enforcement of all *ipso facto* clauses).

Whether acceleration (and, in particular, contractual acceleration) has occurred upon a bankruptcy filing affects the right to a make-whole premium.

21.5 What arguments have been made for and against the allowance of make-whole claims?

The arguments center around three themes: (1) whether the language of the indenture entitles the holders to a make-whole premium; (2) whether the premium is a penalty or liquidated damages; and (3) whether the make-whole premium is disallowable as unmatured interest.

The arguments most often asserted by issuers and the counter-arguments by indenture trustees are summarized as follows:

> 1. A make-whole premium is due only if the securities are repaid before the maturity date. Bankruptcy accelerates the debt securities; accordingly, principal and accrued interest are immediately due and payable, and thus maturity has occurred.
>
> **RESPONSE**: Bankruptcy does not automatically accelerate the obligation because the acceleration that occurs when a bankruptcy is filed is only for purposes of a creditor filing a proof of claim. Bankruptcy does not operate as a voluntary or contractual acceleration by the holders.
>
> 2. If the indenture provides for automatic acceleration upon the filing of a bankruptcy, this conclusively negates the entitlement to a make-whole premium because maturity occurs upon acceleration.

RESPONSE: Contractual language providing for automatic acceleration is not enforceable because it is an *ipso facto* clause which is unenforceable under the Bankruptcy Code. Moreover, the holders have a right to decelerate.

3. Even if the holders have the right to decelerate the automatic acceleration, the deceleration would violate the automatic stay.

RESPONSE: To the extent the automatic stay applies, the bankruptcy court should lift the stay.

4. A make-whole premium is only due in an optional or voluntary redemption. Payments during bankruptcy, particularly under a plan, are not optional, nor are they redemptions.

RESPONSE: Chapter 11 allows a debtor to reinstate the indenture, including the maturity date, under a plan. A debtor's election to repay the securities instead of reinstating the indenture is optional. Thus, the holders are entitled to a make-whole premium when the issuer elects to repay the securities instead of reinstating the indenture.

5. A make-whole premium constitutes unmatured interest, and therefore is disallowed under Bankruptcy Code § 502(b)(2).

RESPONSE: If the debtor is solvent, the general rule disallowing unmatured interest under Bankruptcy Code § 502(b)(2) should not apply.

Whether or not the debtor is solvent, the make-whole provision is a valid damages provision, not unmatured interest.

6. The make-whole premium is disproportionate with actual damages and thus is a penalty.

RESPONSE: The make-whole premium is not a penalty but is a liquidated damages provision. Holders are entitled to damages for breach of the call limitations in the indenture and/or for loss of the benefit of the bargain, *i.e.*, lost of interest payments over the term of the securities. The measure of this claim is the amount of the make-whole premium in the indenture, which represents the actual loss of contractually agreed interest over the term and is a valid liquidated damages provision.

7. A make-whole premium, like other prepayment premiums, is not allowed in the absence of language in the indenture requiring the payment after a bankruptcy.

RESPONSE: The inclusion of the word "premium" in the default waterfall reflects the intent that the make-whole premium is payable after a bankruptcy.

8. The absence of explicit language in the indenture stating that holders are entitled to a make-whole premium in a bankruptcy negates the entitlement to a make-whole premium in a bankruptcy.

RESPONSE: The rule of explicitness does not apply to make-whole premiums. To the extent the indenture is ambiguous, it should be construed against the issuer under the doctrine of *contra proferentem*.

21.6 How have the bankruptcy courts analyzed make-whole claims?

Several different lines of analysis have been adopted by courts considering the question of whether to allow a make-whole premium in a bankruptcy case.

The starting point in most cases is the language of the indenture. The cases are fact-specific, turning often on the precise language of the indenture and the facts surrounding the bankruptcy filing and the proposed repayment.

The courts first look at whether the claim would be valid under non-bankruptcy law, and then examine whether there is any limitation or provision for disallowance under the Bankruptcy Code.

Many courts have denied make-whole claims, although the reasoning has not been the same in all the cases. The trend in the Southern District of New York, an important venue for chapter 11 cases, and the Second Circuit, in which the Southern District of New York resides, has been against the allowance of make-whole claims. *In re AMR Corp.*, 730 F.3d at 103-04; *In re MPM Silicones, LLC,* 531 B.R. 321, 335 (S.D.N.Y. 2015). *See also, In re Solutia Inc.*, 379 B.R. at 488-89 (disallowing a claim for breach of a no-call provision); *HSBC Bank USA, N.A. v. Calpine Corp.*, No. 07 Civ 3088(GBD), 2010 WL 3835200, at *3-4 (S.D.N.Y. Sept. 15, 2010) (disallowing a claim for breach of a no-call provision).

Other courts, primarily outside of the Second Circuit, have upheld, or approved the payment of, make-whole claims. *In re School Specialty, Inc.*, No. 13-10125(KJC), 2013 WL 1838513, at *5 (Bankr. D. Del. April 22, 2013), *citing In re Trico Marine Servs., Inc.*, 450 B.R. 474, 479 (Bankr. D. Del. 2011). *See also In re Chemtura Corp.*, 439 B.R. 561, 596 (Bankr. S.D.N.Y. 2010); *In re Premier Entm't Biloxi LLC,* 445 B.R. 582, 633-34 (Bankr. S.D. Miss. 2010).

21.7 What is the procedure by which make-whole disputes are resolved in bankruptcy court?

The entitlement to a make-whole premium is generally brought to the bankruptcy court for determination in an adversary proceeding seeking a declaratory judgment. The action may be brought either by the indenture trustee or the debtor.

The determination of entitlement often turns on the language of the indenture. There are often no disputed facts, at least not as to the facts that the court deems necessary to make a decision. Thus, the case is often decided upon summary judgment motions filed by each side. The court can often make a determination as to the make-whole as a legal matter, without the need for a trial.

21.8 What kind of factual issues arise in make-whole disputes?

A threshold issue in the litigation is usually the language of the indenture. Courts generally will not allow a make-whole premium absent indenture language that entitles the holders to a make-whole premium notwithstanding the issuer's bankruptcy filing or bankruptcy acceleration. Often, the language is ambiguous, at least arguably. The indenture trustee may seek to introduce parol evidence regarding the intent of the parties. As the indenture trustee is not involved in the negotiation of the make-whole provision — very often, these provisions are formulated by the underwriter or issuer and not negotiated at all — the indenture trustee may seek to offer expert testimony as to the expectations of investors in the market at the time. Other factual issues may be raised as to the debtor's solvency, as solvency is often a factor the courts will consider in allowing a make-whole claim.

21.9 What steps must the indenture trustee take in connection with a make-whole premium?

A make-whole premium is usually a material element of the securities to holders.

Following an event of default, the indenture trustee has the duty to act as a prudent person. As a prudent person, the indenture trustee should preserve the right to assert a make-whole claim.

Voluntary acceleration is usually fatal to a make-whole claim. Most trustees will not accelerate under an indenture that contains a make-whole provision, as least not without a direction and indemnification by holders of a majority of the outstanding principal securities.

Most indentures (whether or not they contain a make-whole premium) do not require the indenture trustee to accelerate. Except for its effect on the entitlement to a make-whole premium, acceleration is largely irrelevant once an issuer files bankruptcy. This is because the Bankruptcy Code provides that a creditor (including a trustee under a pre-petition indenture) may assert the entire obligation in its proof of claim, whether or not all amounts have become due and owing.

PRACTICE TIP

Most often, the redemption or repayment that triggers the make-whole claim will not occur until after the debtor's chapter 11 case is filed. A make-whole premium is calculated according to a formula in the indenture as of the date of the optional redemption, prepayment or other early payment, which is usually effectuated either under a confirmed plan or under a court order sought by the debtor. The early payment date may not be known at the time the indenture trustee files its proof of claim.

The proof of claim should reserve the right to assert the make-whole premium, but should contain appropriate reservations so as not to trigger defenses to the make-whole claim, such as acceleration. Some examples of such protective language are:

> This proof of claim encompasses all amounts owed by the Issuer arising under or relating to the Notes or obligations arising under the Indenture, whether contingent or non-contingent, whenever arising, due or owing currently or in the future, as described in this proof of claim, including, but not limited to, principal, interest, fees, costs, expenses, disbursements, indemnifications, premiums, and any obligations of any kind.
>
> This proof of claim is being asserted for purposes of preserving and presenting all claims for allowance in the Issuer's bankruptcy cases, and is not to be deemed an admission or waiver of any kind or on any issue, including without limitation, any claims, defenses or other issues that have been, may be or could have been raised in any law suit, action, proceeding, contested matter, or case brought or which could be brought in this court or any other court or tribunal.

Chapter 22. Intercreditor and Subordination Disputes

22.1 What is an intercreditor agreement?

An intercreditor agreement is an agreement among creditors (*e.g.*, different tranches of debt securities holders or lenders) setting forth the relative rights of each creditor. Intercreditor agreements establish lien or payment priorities (or both) among and between different tranches of debt securities and/or lenders, and specify which remedial actions may or may not be taken by each tranche. Both the indenture trustee and holders of the debt securities are typically parties to an intercreditor agreement.

22.2 What is the difference between an intercreditor agreement and an agreement among lenders ("AAL")?

An AAL is often seen in unitranche financing, in which senior and subordinated notes are issued under one instrument. Unlike an intercreditor agreement in multi-tranche financing, the obligor is often not a party to an AAL.

An AAL provides that upon default, there is one holder who can direct the indenture trustee on behalf of all the security holders. In unitranche arrangements, intercreditor disputes are limited dramatically, although not always completely avoided. *See In re American Roads LLC,* 496 B.R. 727, 732 (Bankr. S.D.N.Y. 2013).

22.3 What is the difference between an intercreditor agreement and a subordination provision?

A subordination provision is a form of intercreditor agreement incorporated in an unsecured, subordinated indenture, and provides that, after an event of default, the rights of the subordinated holders are subject to the rights of the senior holders to be paid in full before the subordinated holders receive any payment.

22.4 What is the difference between lien subordination and payment subordination?

Payment subordination (also called debt subordination) prohibits the junior holders from receiving payment until the senior holders are paid in full. In other words, the junior holders' rights to receive payment are subordinated.

Lien subordination means that the lien of the senior secured creditor has priority over the lien of the junior secured creditor. Lien subordination prevents the payment of proceeds of shared collateral to the junior secured creditor until the senior secured creditor has been paid in full.

Payment subordination is almost always present in a subordinated indenture but is not always present in an intercreditor agreement between first and second lien creditors. An intercreditor agreement among secured parties usually contains lien subordination, providing for priority of liens in shared collateral as well priority in rights to collateral proceeds. Collateral proceeds can be so broadly defined as to be tantamount to a payment priority.

Notwithstanding payment subordination provisions in a subordinated indenture, the issuer's obligations vis-a-vis the senior and subordinated debt securities are sometimes in *pari passu*. In such cases, the issuer is obligated to make a distribution on account of both obligations on a *pro rata* basis, but the trustee under the subordinated indenture will be obligated to turn over the distribution made on account of the subordinated debt securities to the trustee under the senior indenture, until and unless the senior debt securities are paid in full.

22.5 What types of provisions do intercreditor agreements contain?

The agreement will specify certain actions that may not be taken by the junior secured party, as well as actions that are expressly permitted.

Most intercreditor agreements prohibit any junior secured party from:

- Receiving payment from or using proceeds of collateral until all obligations owed to the senior secured party are paid in full
- Challenging the lien of a senior secured party
- Objecting to adequate protection provided to the senior secured party
- Objecting to a cash collateral order consented to by the senior secured party

Some intercreditor agreements prohibit the junior secured party from:

- Objecting to a plan to which the senior secured party consents
- Objecting to an asset sale pursuant to Bankruptcy Code § 363 to which the senior secured party consents

Many intercreditor agreements allow the following actions by junior secured parties:

- Filing an involuntary bankruptcy petition against the issuer
- Seeking appointment of examiner or trustee in a bankruptcy of issuer
- Payment of the junior secured party from non-collateral funds

Most intercreditor agreements permit the following actions by junior parties:

- Filing proofs of claim
- Asserting rights as unsecured creditors
- Serving on a Committee

22.6 What are the implications to the indenture trustee of an intercreditor agreement?

While the economic impact of an intercreditor agreement or a subordination agreement is primarily on the affected creditors (*i.e.*, holders), the indenture trustee is generally bound by the agreements and is responsible for implementing their terms with respect to payment priorities.

The indenture trustee must comply with the intercreditor agreement. This means not taking action which violates the agreement, for example, objecting to a cash collateral or an adequate protection order to which the senior secured creditors have consented, or challenging the senior secured creditors' liens, if those actions are proscribed by the intercreditor agreement. Violating an intercreditor agreement can lead to a lawsuit filed by the senior secured creditors' representative (*e.g.*, an indenture trustee) against the junior creditor's representative (*e.g.*, an indenture trustee).

22.7 What is the effect of a bankruptcy filing on an indenture trustee's obligations under an intercreditor agreement or a subordination provision in an indenture?

Subordination agreements are generally enforceable in bankruptcy cases. See 11 U.S.C. § 510. Notwithstanding section 510, some courts have held that certain basic bankruptcy rights cannot be waived or abridged even by agreement, such as the right to vote on a plan, *see In re 203 N. LaSalle St. Partnership*, 246 B.R. 325, 329-30 (Bankr. N.D. Ill. 2000), but otherwise, intercreditor agreements have been generally enforced. The courts tend to interpret intercreditor agreements between senior and junior secured parties strictly, and interpret ambiguities in favor of junior secured parties. *In re MPM Silicones, LLC*, 531 B.R. at 336.

22.8 May a trustee sue and be sued under intercreditor agreements?

Yes. An indenture trustee is often a party to and/or bound by an intercreditor agreement. In a typical intercreditor agreement between first lien creditors and second lien creditors — which sometimes includes both first lien lenders and/or first lien debt securities holders, and second lien debt security holders — the indenture trustees for each tranche of debt securities are included in the definition of secured party representatives which are parties to the agreement.

For example, in an intercreditor agreement between first lien and second lien holders, the second lien secured party representatives, including the indenture trustee, are prohibited from taking actions inconsistent with the priority lien position of the first lien parties, such as challenging the liens of the first lien parties in a bankruptcy of the issuer or other actions prohibited by the agreement. An indenture trustee for the first lien holders may enforce these provisions by filing a suit. Conversely, an indenture trustee for the second lien holders may be sued for an alleged or threatened breach of intercreditor agreement provisions.

22.9 Under what circumstances might an indenture trustee sue another indenture trustee?

An indenture trustee may sue another indenture trustee to enforce an intercreditor agreement or a subordination provision in an indenture. The suit will typically be brought solely in the representative capacity of each: the plaintiff will bring the case solely in its capacity as indenture trustee and not individually, against the defendant solely in its capacity as indenture trustee and not individually. This is because indenture trustees are each parties to an intercreditor agreement, not individually but in their respective representative capacities.

While intercreditor litigation is sometimes brought by senior holders against junior holders, litigation involving subordination provisions of an indenture are almost always brought by one trustee against another, in each instance, seeking a declaratory judgment under the subordination provision.

An indenture trustee's actions in a bankruptcy case could trigger litigation under an intercreditor agreement, and that litigation might be brought by another trustee. A first lien indenture trustee might bring suit against a second lien indenture trustee to enjoin actions in a bankruptcy case violating the intercreditor agreement, such as actions challenging the first lien holders' liens. Another dispute which arises is whether the senior creditor under an intercreditor agreement is entitled to amounts which are disallowed by the bankruptcy court against the debtor (such as a make-whole premium or post-petition interest) before junior creditors are entitled to any distribution from the bankruptcy estate. These disputes often involve the question of whether the rule of explicitness applies. This rule provides that the language must be explicit in order for the senior creditors to be entitled to payment of post-petition interest before junior creditors are entitled to a distribution.

An event that often precipitates a suit is a payment (such as an adequate protection payment) or distribution by the debtor which is subject to claims by both trustees. Examples are:

- A plan distribution to a second lien trustee, which the first lien trustee asserts are proceeds of collateral in which the first lien trustee has a priority;
- Secured parties with the same priority dispute the allocation of payments under an intercreditor agreement; or
- A distribution of securities which the senior notes indenture trustee claims must be turned over to it under the subordination provision but which the subordinated notes indenture trustee claims are excluded from turnover under an "X-Clause."

22.10 What is an X-Clause?

The subordination provision typically contains an exception (the "X-Clause") that allows junior note holders, in a chapter 11 plan, to receive and retain securities that are subordinate to the consideration being given to the senior note holders, to the same extent as the existing subordination. While this concept sounds straightforward, in actual application it is not. Both the meaning and application of X-Clauses have been vigorously litigated.

22.11 Why does litigation arise over the meaning and application of an X-Clause?

X-Clauses are common in subordinated indentures, but the wording varies and is almost always unclear. For example, consider the X-Clause wording in *In re Dura Automotive Systems, Inc.*, 379 B.R. 257 (Bankr. D. Del. 2007):

> **Section 10.02. Liquidation; Dissolution; Bankruptcy.**
>
> Upon any distribution to creditors of the Company in a liquidation or dissolution of the Company, in a bankruptcy, reorganization, insolvency, receivership or similar proceeding relating to the Company or its property, in an assignment for the benefit of creditors or in any marshalling of the Company's assets and liabilities:
>
> (i) holders of Senior Debt shall be entitled to receive payment in full of all Obligations due in respect of such Senior Debt (including interest after the commencement of any such proceeding at the rate specified in the applicable Senior Debt) before

Holders of the Notes shall be entitled to receive any payment with respect to the Notes (except that Holders may receive (i) Permitted Junior Securities and (ii) payments and other distributions made from any defeasance trust created pursuant to Section 8.01 hereof); and

(ii) until all Obligations with respect to Senior Debt (as provided in subsection (i) above) are paid in full, any distribution to which Holders would be entitled but for this Article 10 shall be made to the holders of Senior Debt (except that Holders of Notes may receive (i) Permitted Junior Securities and (ii) payments and other distributions made from any defeasance trust created pursuant to Section 8.01 hereof), as their interests may appear.

See Subordinated Notes Indenture, § 10.03 (adding emphasis to the language at issue, known as the "X-Clause")....

"Permitted Junior Securities" means:

(1) Equity Interests in the Company. . . ; or

(2) debt securities that are subordinated to all Senior Debt and any debt securities issued in exchange for Senior Debt to substantially the same extent as, or to a greater extent than, the Notes and the Guaranties are subordinated to Senior Debt under this Indenture.

See Subordinated Notes Indenture, § 1.01.
Id. at 261.

The language, read literally, defines equity interests in the debtor as "Permitted Junior Securities" which subordinated holders are allowed to retain. Because the two parts of the definition, (1) and (2), are disjunctive — connected by "or" not "and" — each stands alone. Read literally, the qualifying language in (2) does not modify (1). Thus, the literal reading supports the subordinated trustee's position. Nevertheless, the court in *Dura* rejected the literal and grammatical reading, *citing In re Envirodyne Indus., Inc.*, 161 B.R. 440, 447 (Bankr. N.D. Ill. 1993), *aff'd*, 29 F.3d 301 (7th Cir. 1994) and *In re PWS Holding Corp.*, 228 F.3d 224, 244-45 (3d Cir. 2000).

The X-Clause in each of these cases was badly drafted, and, as Judge Carey noted in *Dura*, "lacked utter clarity." In fact, read literally, each X-Clause said exactly the opposite of how each court interpreted it. Stated simply, courts have uniformly rejected the literal reading of badly written X-Clauses on the basis that a literal reading would eviscerate the purpose of the subordination clause. *In re PWS Holding Corp., supra.*; *In re Metromedia Fiber Network, Inc.*, 416 F.3d 136, 139-40 (2d Cir. 2005), *In re Envirodyne Indus., Inc., supra*, and *In re Adelphia Communications Corp.*, No. 02-41729, J. Gerber, at p.55 (Bankr. S.D.N.Y. April 6, 2006).

Rejecting a literal reading of an X-Clause has often required a departure from widely accepted semantic and syntactic rules of language. The *Dura* court — construing an "or" as an "and" — wrote:

> Considering the X-Clause before me, I conclude that it must not be considered based upon its grammatical structure alone, but also within the context of the entire agreement, which, here, is more reflective of the parties' intent: that except in very limited circumstances, no payment can be made to the Subordinated Noteholders until (1) the Senior Notes are paid in full, or (2) the Senior Noteholders consent.

In re Dura, 379 B.R. at 270.

The Model Indenture proposes a straightforward and clear formulation of the subordination provision in a subordinated indenture, including an alternative to the traditional, convoluted X-Clause:

> **Section 11.13. Exception for Certain Distributions**
>
> The rights of holders of Senior Debt under this Article do not extend (a) to any Distribution to the extent applied to the Trustee's rights to compensation, reimbursement of expenses or indemnification or (b) to (i) securities which are subordinated to the securities distributed to the holders of Senior Debt on terms no less favorable to the holders of Senior Debt than the provisions of this Article, or (ii) Distributions under any plan approved by the court in any Proceeding.

The Model Indenture language offers clarity and presents an avenue for resolving subordination issues in a plan of reorganization. Use of this provision would likely lead to less litigation and more negotiated resolutions.

PRACTICE TIP

Never underestimate the importance of the "hold-up problem" in economics. The hold-up problem refers to a situation when one side has more invested than the other, giving the side with less investment more leverage. This can occur when one side has a stronger legal position but the other side has nothing to lose, creating an asymmetrical negotiation. This often occurs in a chapter 11 case, and specifically in the situation where one or more tranches of securities are completely "out of the money."

Bankruptcy courts recognize the widespread use of hold-up value. As Judge Gerber wrote in *In re Adelphia Communications, Corp.*, 359 B.R. 54, 63 (Bankr. S.D.N.Y. 2006),

> "... a culture has developed in large chapter 11 cases in which many consider it acceptable, and indeed expected, to use the litigation process as a means to assert or follow through on threats, and to seek various kinds of relief, to secure "leverage"in efforts to increase recoveries."

The hold-up problem is often confronted by indenture trustees in intercreditor disputes. Litigation consumes time, energy, and resources to defend and resolve, all of which will affect holders.

Sometimes hold-up value can increase holders' recovery. Trustees under subordinated or second lien indentures are presented with the dilemma of whether to expend resources to exert hold-up value. Commencing litigation to exert hold-up value is inherently speculative and sometimes risky, but it can also be productive.

Indenture trustees may pursue litigation when doing so has a reasonable chance of bringing about a better resolution for holders, even if the trustee's chances of prevailing in court are not strong. Before undertaking such litigation, trustees will typically:

1. Solicit the views of holders through a notice, which may include the scheduling of a holder conference call to discuss the proposed course of action.

2. Seek advice and recommendation of counsel, including analysis of the claim and costs and risks associated with the action.
3. Obtain internal review as appropriate under corporate trust department policies.
4. Seek direction and indemnification if the trustee deems it necessary.

22.12 What context gives rise to intercreditor suits brought by or against an indenture trustee?

It is rare that litigation ensues over actions that are either clearly allowed or prohibited by an intercreditor agreement. Creditor representatives, and particularly indenture trustees, will not generally violate the clear language in an intercreditor agreement, even if directed to. Where an indenture trustee takes actions in what might be called a "grey area" — where the agreement is ambiguous — such actions are more likely to elicit a lawsuit.

An example of such a grey area is the circumstance in which the holders' claims are undersecured or even completely unsecured and, consequently, the second lien indenture trustee is serving on a Committee. Committees are adverse (as a general proposition) to senior second creditors. A Committee examines the validity or perfection of the liens of secured creditors as part of the Committee's role and responsibility in a chapter 11 case. Many intercreditor agreements expressly permit a second lien indenture trustee to serve on a Committee to protect its rights as an unsecured creditor, but prohibit the second lien trustee from directly undertaking a lien challenge or objecting to the adequate protection afforded a first lien creditor.

In situations in which second lien indenture trustees not only serve on, but dominate the Committee, and in which the Committee takes action that the indenture trustee does not have the right to take under the intercreditor agreement, a first lien indenture trustee could potentially claim that the intercreditor agreement is violated. Such a claim may be hard to sustain for a number of reasons. Committee deliberations and votes are private, privileged, and subject to a limited immunity. Moreover, ambiguity in intercreditor agreements is usually resolved against senior lien holders. However, in a given case, the first lien indenture trustee may determine that it is prudent to file suit to attempt to constrain the activities. At the same time, the second lien trustee may deem it prudent to support a lien challenge by the Committee. This is a situation faced uniquely by second lien indenture trustees in situations where the holders are undersecured. No other creditor representative has a duty to act as a prudent person, making its Committee role not entirely optional.

PRACTICE TIP

The indenture trustee is entitled to seek the advice and recommendations of counsel before filing an action against another trustee in connection with an X-Clause or intercreditor agreement.

Some intercreditor agreements and X-Clause provisions are not perfectly clear, and indeed are susceptible of more than one interpretation. Courts have tended, in considering an intercreditor agreement involving secured creditors, to interpret ambiguity in favor of the junior creditors. *See, e.g.*, *In re MPM Silicones, LLC*, Case No. 14-22503 rrd, 2014 WL 4436335 (Bankr. S.D.N.Y. Sept. 9, 2014). With respect to interpretation of X-Clauses, however, the trend has gone in the opposite direction: ambiguities have been resolved against the subordinated holders and in favor of the senior holders. *See In re Dura*, 379 B.R. at 270.

Nevertheless, there is almost always room to advance arguments contrary to the trend in the X-Clause cases based on the particular facts of a case, the specific language of the indenture, and the non-precedential nature of an unfavorable prior decision.

Counsel for the indenture trustee should consider all of these factors in formulating a recommendation.

22.13 May a party seeking to enforce its rights under an intercreditor agreement in a bankruptcy case file an action to enforce those rights in a non-bankruptcy court?

Yes, subject to certain limitations. First, any suit which names the debtor as a defendant in intercreditor litigation must be brought in bankruptcy court unless the plaintiff first obtains relief from the automatic stay. Relief from the stay is rarely granted in these circumstances.

A suit only against non-debtor parties (such as the indenture trustee or holders) can be brought in a venue specified in the intercreditor agreement. If the suit involves or implicates the bankruptcy case, any of the parties, including the indenture trustee, may remove the suit to the federal district court in the district in which the suit was filed. 28 U.S.C. § 1452(a); Fed. R. Bankr. P. 9027 (a)(1). A party may move to remand the case. 28 U.S.C. § 1452(b); Fed. R. Bankr. P. 9027(d).

Chapter 23. Anti-Impairment Litigation

23.1 What is the anti-impairment provision?

The anti-impairment provision refers to an indenture provision reflecting section 316(b) of the TIA, which states as follows:

> Notwithstanding any other provision of the indenture to be qualified, the right of any holder of any indenture security to receive payment of the principal of and interest on such indenture security, on or after the respective due dates expressed in such indenture security, or to institute suit for the enforcement of any such payment on or after such respective dates, shall not be impaired or affected without the consent of such holder, except as to a postponement of an interest payment consented to in paragraph (2) of subsection (a) of this section, and except that such indenture may contain a provision limiting or denying the right of any such holder to institute any such suit, if and to the extent that the institution or prosecution thereof or the entry of the judgment therein would, under applicable law result in the surrender, impairment, waiver, or loss of the lien of such indenture upon any property subject to such lien.

This section was intended to protect individual holders' rights to principal and interest. *See, e.g., Upic & Co. v. Kinder-Care Learning Ctrs., Inc.*, 793 F. Supp. 448, 452 (S.D.N.Y. 1992) ("Section 316(b) expressly prohibits use of an indenture that permits modification by majority securityholder vote of any core term of the indenture, *i.e.*, one affecting a securityholder's right to receive payment of the principal of or interest on the indenture security on the due dates for such payments . . . .").

Section 316(b) is typically incorporated into TIA-qualified indentures using language along the lines of Model Indenture, section 6.07:

> **Section 6.07. Rights of Holders To Receive Payment.**
>
> Notwithstanding any other provision of this Indenture, the right of any Holder of a Security to receive payment of Principal and interest on the Security, on or after the respective due dates expressed in the Security, or to bring suit for the enforcement of any such payment on or after such respective dates, shall not be impaired or affected without the consent of the Holder.

Section 316(b) is deemed to be included in every TIA-qualified indenture whether or not specifically set forth in the indenture. TIA § 318(c).

23.2 What kinds of actions or modifications are prohibited by anti-impairment provisions and section 316(b)?

The precise scope of actions or modifications prohibited by section 316(b) is not well defined, and the interpretation of this section has evolved dramatically. The predominant view for several decades since enactment has been that section 316(b) was a narrow provision that prevented the modification of core terms, *i.e.*, the payment terms of the indenture.

The United States District Court for the Southern District of New York has interpreted section 316(b) as limiting the ability of an issuer to conduct an exchange offer or consent solicitation, or to effectuate amendments to the indenture which affect the ability of a holder to obtain payment of principal and interest. *Marblegate Asset Mgmt., LLC v. Education Mgmt. Corp.*, No. 14 Civ. 8584(KPF), 2015 WL 3867643 (S.D.N.Y. June 23, 2015). *MeehanCombs Global Credit Opportunities Funds, L.P. v. Caesars Entm't Corp.*, Nos. 14-cv-7091 (SAS), 14-cv-7973 (SAS), 2015 WL 221055 (S.D.N.Y. Jan. 15, 2015). These decisions construed section 316(b) in the context of an out-of-court restructuring of notes issued under a TIA-governed indenture, in which a parent guarantee was released and/or assets of the issuer were being transferred out of the reach of note holders. In each instance, the release or transfer was allowed under the literal terms of the indenture, and was effectuated by the consent of holders with less than 100% of the outstanding notes.

The *Marblegate* and *MeehanCombs* decisions stand for the propositions that:

- TIA Section 316(b) protects not only a holder's legal right to principal and interest but also the practical ability to obtain payment.
- An out-of-court restructuring which impairs the ability of holders which did not consent to the restructuring to obtain payment as a practical matter — such as by leaving them with an insolvent issuer — may violate TIA Section 316(b), even when core terms are not amended.

Prior to these decisions, section 316(b) and anti-impairment provisions were viewed as preventing an issuer from affecting the holders' legal right to sue for principal and interest but not protecting holders' practical ability to obtain payment. This view has changed based on the opinions in *Marblegate* and *MeehanCombs*. These cases suggest that even if an indenture permits the release of guarantors or the transfer of assets with less than 100% consent of holders, such an action may be invalid if it is part of an out-of-court restructuring and impairs a non-consenting holder's ability to obtain payment of principal and interest.

Marblegate and *MeehanCombs* are groundbreaking decisions which cast doubt on any material modification of an indenture by a distressed issuer, or by an issuer in connection with an out-of-court restructuring.

23.3 What factual situations give rise to a potential violation of section 316(b)?

There is no bright line test under the current case law, but the facts in *Marblegate* and *Meehan-Combs* are instructive. One threshold event is the fact that modifications or amendments were effectuated as a part of a restructuring.

The defendant in the *Marblegate* case, Education Management Corp., had valid reasons for pursuing an out of court restructuring instead of a chapter 11 bankruptcy: a bankruptcy would have rendered it ineligible for Title IV funds which comprised most of its revenue. Education Management Corp. was the guarantor of unsecured notes issued by its subsidiary, Education Management, LLC.

Education Management negotiated an agreement with a group of holders that held a large majority of both unsecured notes and secured debt. The agreement gave the rest of the holders a choice of either exchanging their notes for new equity representing a recovery of only about one-third on their existing notes, or retaining their old notes.

The holders who did not agree to the exchange would be left with the following scenario: the assets of the subsidiary would be foreclosed upon by the secured lenders and transferred to the parent, which would have been released under the indenture — leaving the holders with claims against a subsidiary with no assets. The release would occur under an indenture provision releasing the parent if the parent's guarantee of secured debt was released. At the time of the note issuance, no such guarantee of secured debt existed, but one was put into place at the time of the restructuring, ostensibly to create a "carrot and stick" approach to the minority holders.

The court posed the key question succinctly:

> The question put before the Court is straightforward: does a debt restructuring violate Section 316(b) of the Trust Indenture Act when it does not modify any indenture term explicitly governing the right to receive interest or principal on a certain date, yet leaves bondholders no choice but to accept a modification of the terms of their bonds? Examining the text, history, and purpose of the Trust Indenture Act, the Court concludes that the answer is yes.

Marblegate, at *3.

The court ruled that Education Management's restructuring violated Marblegate's rights under the TIA and held that Education Management was obligated for any past and future payments of principal and interest to Marblegate under the indenture.[11]

Marblegate, at *14.

In *MeehanCombs*, the plaintiffs, holders of unsecured notes issued by Caesars Entertainment Operating Company (CEOC) and guaranteed by its parent, Caesars Entertainment Corporation (CEC), lost their only meaningful source for recovery when CEC was released from its guarantee via exit consents by a group of holders whose notes were purchased by Caesars. Caesars purchased those notes from a group of holders on terms favorable to these holders (par plus accrued interest — a huge premium over the market for the notes at the time) in exchange for their agreement to release CEC's guarantee and modify certain indenture covenants restricting disposition of CEOC's assets. The removal of covenants allowed Caesars to continue to strip assets from CEOC.

The *MeehanCombs* plaintiffs alleged that for several years prior to the note purchase, CEOC transferred valuable assets to CEC with the intent of removing them from the reach of CEOC's creditors. Unlike Education Management, Caesars did not make its offer to purchase notes on favorable terms to all holders; the *MeehanCombs* plaintiffs were not given any options with respect to their notes.

The plaintiff's suit asserted breach of the indenture and violation of TIA § 316 (b). In its denial of the defendant's motion to dismiss, the court called the removal of the CEC guarantee "an impermissible out-of-court debt restructuring achieved through collective action. This is exactly what TIA section 316 (b) is designed to prevent." *MeehanCombs,* 2015 WL 221055, at 5.

PRACTICE TIP

If the trustee is requested to sign a supplemental indenture in connection with an exchange offer containing indenture amendments that may violate section 316(b), the trustee and/or its counsel should:

- Review the consent solicitation statement/offering document and discuss with the issuer's counsel whether the proposed amendments violate section 316(b).
- Determine whether the indenture trustee is required to sign the supplemental indenture or whether the amendment can become effective without the trustee's signature.
- Determine whether the amendment can be effected without the consent of 100% of the holders.

- Request an officers' certificate and opinion of counsel that includes federal law (*i.e.* an opinion that the amendment does not violate the TIA).
- Request an indemnity, if the indenture entitles the trustee to one.
- Ensure that all notices and other documents required under the indenture are provided.

If there is any uncertainty as to whether the amendment violates the TIA, the indenture trustee may decide to seek a declaratory judgment from a court of appropriate jurisdiction.

23.4 Does an indenture trustee have the right to file an action for a violation of TIA § 316 (b)?

Yes. The indenture trustee has a right to enforce the indenture. Rights under TIA § 316(b) are inherent in any TIA-governed indenture — whether or not expressly stated in the indenture. TIA § 318(c). Accordingly, violation of TIA § 316(b) is a breach of the indenture which may be enforced by the trustee.

PRACTICE TIP

The TIA-litigation described in this Chapter is ongoing. As of the writing of this book, the *Marblegate* decision is on appeal, and when final decisions are entered in *MeehanCombs* and related lawsuits, they will likely be appealed as well. It is anticipated that the United States Court of Appeals for the Second Circuit will review decisions in both *Marblegate* and *MeehanCombs*, and thus the discussion in this book will likely require supplementation at a later time. Updates will be available on the *INDENTURE TRUSTEE Bankruptcy Powers & Duties* website at indenturetrustee.nyc.

ENDNOTES

[1] The TIA is applicable "to notes, bonds, debentures, and other evidences of indebtedness, whether or not secured, and to all certificates representing such an interest." 6 Thomas Lee Hazen, Securities Regulation § 19.2 (2015), *available at* Westlaw 6 Law Sec. Reg. 19.2. The legislative history of the TIA indicates that because "previous abuses by indenture trustees had adversely affected 'the national public interest and the interest of investors in notes, bonds [and] debentures,' 15 U.S.C. § 77bbb (a)," "Congress sought to address this national problem in a uniform way." *Bluebird Partners, L.P. v. First Fidelity Bank, N.A. N.J.*, 85 F.3d 970, 974 (2d Cir. 1996), *citing* S. Rep. No 248, 76th Cong., 1st Sess. 3 (1939) (alteration in original). In short, "[t]he Act is designed to vindicate a federal policy of protecting investors." *Id.* (internal quotations, citations, and emphasis omitted).

[2] A court may be less likely to uphold choice of law provisions with respect to common law claims, such as a breach of fiduciary duty, especially if the provision is not broadly drafted to encompass the entirety of the parties' relationship. *See Taylor v. U.S. Bank, N.A.*, CIVIL ACTION H-12-3550, 2015 U.S. Dist. LEXIS 14194, at *11-17 (S.D. Tex. Feb. 6, 2015).

[3] The American Bar Foundation of the American Bar Association published a model debenture indenture in 1965. This model has been rarely used since the publication of the subsequent models.

[4] The TIA provides narrow exceptions in the instance that a stay is obtained from the SEC.

[5] This is commonly called a "tripartite agreement." An example of a tripartite agreement is set forth at Appendix A.

[6] Section 310(b) of the TIA requires an indenture trustee to provide notice to holders if it fails to resign within 90 days of ascertaining that it has a conflicting interest.

[7] In some cases, debtors will obtain blanket authorization to settle certain types of claims or objections — for example, where the claim or the settlement involves non-material amounts — without court approval or upon limited notice. Such blanket orders are the exception to the general practice whereby claim objections are settled through a Fed. R. Bankr. P 9019 motion or pursuant to a plan.

[8] Generally speaking, a qualified institutional buyer (QIB) is a purchaser that is not an individual, meets certain entity requirements established by the SEC, and owns and invests, on a discretionary basis, at least $100 million in securities, or in the case of certain registered dealers, $10 million. See Securities Act § 144A. The term "accredited investor" is defined in Title 17, Chapter II, Part 230, § 230.501.

[9] Bankruptcy Code § 546(e) provides a "safe harbor" against avoidance as a fraudulent conveyance under § 548(a)(1)(B) for certain transfers in connection with a securities contract made by or to (or for the benefit of) a financial institution. This section has been invoked by financial institutions serving as indenture trustees as a defense to section 548(a)(1)(B) claims. *See In re Quebecor World (USA) Inc.*, 719 F.3d 94, 98 (2d Cir. 2013).

[10] Payment outside a plan of pre-petition claims, such as debt securities, requires bankruptcy court approval after notice and a hearing.

[11] Education Management appealed the decision. As of the date of this writing, the case is on appeal to the United States Court of Appeals for the Second Circuit.

The appendices contain forms of certain documents commonly used by indenture trustees. These are intended only as examples, not as models or prescribed formulations. Each corporate trust institution has its own preferred formulations for these documents which may vary both in form and substance from those appended.

APPENDIX A Tripartite Agreement

AGREEMENT OF RESIGNATION, APPOINTMENT AND ACCEPTANCE (this "**Agreement**"), dated as of December 15, 2015 (the "**Effective Date**"), by and among XYZ ISSUER CORP., a Delaware corporation having an office at 123 Main Street, City, State 00000 ("XYZ"), (the "**Issuer**"), ABC CORPORATE TRUST COMPANY, N.A., a national banking association duly organized and existing under the laws of the United States of America and having an office at 123 Smith Street, City, State 00000, Trustee ("**Resigning Trustee**"), and NOTES & BONDS TRUST COMPANY, a New York banking corporation having an office at 555 Main Street, City, State 00000 in its capacity as successor trustee the ("**Successor Trustee**").

RECITALS:

WHEREAS, Resigning Trustee acts as Trustee under that certain Indenture, dated as of January 1, 2015, among the Issuer and Resigning Trustee (as amended and supplemented the "**Indenture**"), pursuant to which $1,000,000,000 aggregate principal amount of the Issuer's 10% Senior Notes due 2025 (the "**Notes**") were issued and are outstanding as of the date hereof;

WHEREAS, Section 7.08 of the Indenture provides that the Trustee may resign at any time by giving 30 days prior written notice of such resignation (the "**Notice Period**") to the Issuer, effective upon the acceptance by a successor Trustee of its appointment as successor Trustee;

WHEREAS, the Issuer desires to waive the Notice Period;

WHEREAS, Section 7.08 of the Indenture provides that any successor Trustee appointed in accordance with the Indenture shall execute, acknowledge and deliver to the Issuer and to its predecessor Trustee a written acceptance of such appointment under the Indenture, and thereupon the resignation of the predecessor Trustee shall become effective and such successor Trustee, without any further act, deed or conveyance, shall become vested with all rights, powers, duties and obligations of the predecessor Trustee;

WHEREAS, Resigning Trustee was appointed Registrar and Paying Agent and to act as Custodian for the Global Notes by the Issuer pursuant to Section 2.03 of the Indenture;

WHEREAS, the Issuer desires to appoint Successor Trustee as Trustee, Registrar and Paying Agent to succeed Resigning Trustee and to act as Custodian for the Global Notes under the Indenture, whereupon Resigning Trustee shall be discharged from its respective duties and obligations under the Indenture; and

WHEREAS, Successor Trustee is willing to accept such appointments as successor Trustee, Registrar, Paying Agent and Custodian for the Global Notes under the Indenture.

NOW, THEREFORE, the Issuer, Resigning Trustee and Successor Trustee, for and in consideration of the premises and of other good and valuable consideration, the receipt and sufficiency of which are hereby acknowledged, hereby consent and agree as follows:

ARTICLE 1

RESIGNING TRUSTEE

Section 1.01. Pursuant to Section 7.08 of the Indenture, Resigning Trustee notifies the Issuer that Resigning Trustee is hereby resigning as Trustee, Registrar, Paying Agent and Custodian for the Global Notes under the Indenture.

Section 1.02. Resigning Trustee hereby represents and warrants to Successor Trustee that:

(a) No covenant or condition contained in the Indenture has been waived by Resigning Trustee or, to the best of the knowledge of its Responsible Officers, by the Holders of the percentage in aggregate principal amount of the Notes required by the Indenture to effect any such waiver.

(b) There is no action, suit or proceeding pending or, to the best of the knowledge of its Responsible Officers, threatened against it before any court or any governmental authority arising out of any action or omission by it as Trustee under the Indenture.

(c) Each person who authenticated the Notes on behalf of Resigning Trustee was duly elected or appointed, qualified and acting as an officer or authorized signatory of Resigning Trustee and empowered to authenticate the Notes at the respective times of such authentication and the signature of such person or persons appearing on such Notes is each such person's genuine signature.

(d) As of the Effective Date, it holds no property under the Indenture.

(e) As of the Effective Date, (i) $1,000,000,000 aggregate principal amount of Notes are outstanding under the Indenture, all of which were duly authenticated by Resigning Trustee.

(f) This Agreement has been duly authorized, executed and delivered on behalf of the Resigning Trustee it and constitutes the legal, valid and binding obligation, of the Resigning Trustee.

Section 1.03. Resigning Trustee hereby assigns, transfers, delivers and confirms to Successor Trustee all right, title and interest of Resigning Trustee in and to the trusts under the Indenture, and Resigning Trustee hereby assigns, transfers, delivers and confirms to Successor Trustee, all the rights, powers and trusts of the Trustee under the Indenture. Resigning Trustee shall execute and deliver such further instruments and shall take such other actions as Successor Trustee may reasonably request so as to more fully and certainly vest and confirm in Successor Trustee all the rights, trusts and powers hereby assigned, transferred, delivered and confirmed to it as Trustee, Registrar, Paying Agent and Custodian for the Global Notes under the Indenture.

Section 1.04. Resigning Trustee shall deliver to Successor Trustee, as of or immediately after the Effective Date, all of the documents listed on Schedule 1 hereto; provided, however, that Resigning Trustee shall deliver any and all Global Notes to Successor Trustee as soon as practicable following the Effective Date. Thereafter, Resigning Trustee shall deliver all such additional documents with respect to the Notes as Successor Trustee may reasonably request from time to time.

Section 1.05. In the event that after the Effective Date Resigning Trustee (whether in its capacities as Trustee, Registrar, Paying Agent, or Custodian) receives any amounts (other than amounts payable to it in respect of Resigning Trustee's fees, expenses, indemnities or similar payments) in respect of obligations under the Indenture that were intended to be received by Successor Trustee, Resigning Trustee shall promptly after it shall have obtained actual knowledge thereof remit such amounts to Successor Trustee.

ARTICLE 2

THE ISSUER

Section 2.01. The Issuer hereby accepts the resignation of Resigning Trustee as Trustee, Registrar, Paying Agent and Custodian for the Global Notes under the Indenture.

Section 2.02. The Issuer hereby appoints Successor Trustee as Trustee, Registrar, Paying Agent and Custodian for the Global Notes under the Indenture to succeed to, and hereby vest Successor Trustee, with all the rights, powers, duties and obligations of Resigning Trustee under the Indenture, with like effect as if originally named as Trustee in the Indenture.

Section 2.03. The Issuer hereby represents and warrant to Resigning Trustee and Successor Trustee that:

(a) XYZ is a corporation duly formed and validly existing under the laws of the State of Delaware.

(b) The Indenture was validly and lawfully executed and delivered by the Issuer and is in full force and effect, and the Notes were validly issued by the Issuer.

(c) The Issuer has performed or fulfilled prior to the date hereof, and will continue to perform and fulfill after the date hereof, each covenant, agreement, condition, obligation and responsibility on their part to be performed or fulfilled under the Indenture.

(d) This Agreement has been duly authorized, executed and delivered on behalf of Issuer and constitutes the legal, valid and binding obligations of the Issuer.

(e) All covenants and conditions (including any conditions precedent) relating to the appointment of Notes & Bonds Trust Company as successor Trustee under the Indenture have been complied with.

(f) The last interest payment on the Notes was made by the Issuer on June 15, 2015.

(g) Notice has not been given by the Issuer to any of Resigning Trustee's Responsible Officers of an Event of Default or the occurrence of an event that is continuing which is, or after notice or lapse of time would become, an Event of Default under Section 6.01 of the Indenture.

(h) To the best knowledge of the Issuer, no covenant or condition contained in the Indenture has been waived by Resigning Trustee or by the Holders of the percentage in aggregate principal amount of the Notes required by the Indenture to effect any such waiver.

Section 2.04. The Issuer shall execute and deliver such further instruments and shall take such other actions as Successor Trustee may reasonably request so as to more fully and certainly vest and confirm in Successor Trustee all the rights, trusts and powers hereby assigned, transferred, delivered and confirmed to it as Trustee, Registrar, Paying Agent and Custodian for the Global Notes under the Indenture.

ARTICLE 3

SUCCESSOR TRUSTEE

Section 3.01. Successor Trustee hereby represents and warrants to Resigning Trustee and the Issuer that:

(a) Successor Trustee is not disqualified under the provisions of Section 7.10 of the Indenture and is eligible under the provisions of Section 7.10 of the Indenture to act as Trustee under the Indenture.

(b) This Agreement has been duly authorized, executed and delivered on behalf of Successor Trustee and constitutes the legal, valid and binding obligation of Successor Trustee.

Section 3.02. Successor Trustee hereby accepts its appointment as successor Trustee, Registrar, Paying Agent and Custodian for the Global Notes under the Indenture and accepts the rights, powers, duties and obligations of Resigning Trustee as Trustee, Registrar, Paying Agent and Custodian for the Global Notes under the Indenture, upon the terms and conditions set forth therein, with like effect as if originally named as Trustee, Registrar, Paying Agent and Custodian for the Global Notes under the Indenture. Upon the Effective Date, Resigning Trustee (including in its capacity as Registrar, Paying Agent and Custodian for the Global Notes) shall be discharged from all obligations as Trustee, Registrar, Paying Agent and Custodian for the Global Notes under the Indenture in each case, arising after the Effective Date.

Section 3.03. Promptly after the Effective Date, Successor Trustee shall cause a notice, substantially in the form of Schedule 2 hereto, to be sent to each Holder of the Notes in accordance with the provisions of Section 7.08 of the Indenture.

Section 3.04. References in the Indenture to "Corporate Trust Office of the Trustee" or other similar terms shall be deemed to refer to the Corporate Trust Office of Successor Trustee at 555 Main Street, City, State 00000 or any other office of Successor Trustee at which, at any particular time, its corporate trust business shall be administered and which is notified to the Issuer.

ARTICLE 4

MISCELLANEOUS

Section 4.01. Except as otherwise expressly provided herein or unless the context otherwise requires, all terms used herein which are defined in the Indenture shall have the meaning assigned to them in the Indenture.

Section 4.02. This Agreement and the resignation, appointment and acceptance effected hereby shall be effective as of the Effective Date; [provided, however, that the resignation of Resigning Trustee as Paying Agent, Registrar and Custodian for the Global Notes under the Indenture and appointment of Successor Trustee as Paying Agent, Registrar and Custodian for the Global Notes under the Indenture shall be effective as soon as practicable].

Section 4.03. Notwithstanding the resignation of Resigning Trustee effected hereby, the Issuer shall remain obligated to Resigning Trustee to the full extent provided by Section 7.07 of the Indenture, including, for the avoidance of doubt, the obligation to (i) indemnify Resigning Trustee in connection with its prior trusteeship under the Indenture and (ii) reimburse or cause to be reimbursed Resigning Trustee for any unpaid compensation or other amounts owed to Resigning Trustee as set forth in Section 7.07 of the Indenture. The Issuer also acknowledges and affirms its obligations to Successor Trustee as set forth in Section 7.07 of the Indenture.

Section 4.04. This Agreement shall be governed by and construed in accordance with the laws of the State of New York.

Section 4.05. This Agreement may be executed in any number of counterparts each of which shall be an original, but such counterparts shall together constitute but one and the same instrument.

Section 4.06. The Issuer, Resigning Trustee and Successor Trustee hereby acknowledge receipt of an executed and acknowledged counterpart of this Agreement and the effectiveness thereof.

Section 4.07. Any notice or communication by the Issuer, Resigning Trustee or Successor Trustee to the others is duly and timely given if in writing and delivered in person or by first class mail (registered or certified, return receipt requested), facsimile transmission or overnight air courier guaranteeing next day delivery, to the others' address:

If to the Issuer:

XYZ Issuer Corp.
123 Main Street
City, State 00000
Facsimile: 123-123-1234
Attention: General Counsel

With a copy to (which copy shall not constitute notice):

[XYZ Issuer Corp.'s Counsel]
456 Main Street
City, State 00000
Facsimile: 567-567-5678
Attention: John Doe, Esq.

If to Resigning Trustee:

ABC Corporate Trust Company
123 Smith Street
City, State 00000
Facsimile: 111-111-2222
Attention:

With a copy to (which copy shall not constitute notice):
[ABC Corporate Trust Company's Counsel]
345 Smith Street
City, State 00000
Facsimile: 555-555-5656
Attention: Jane Doe, Esq.

If to Successor Trustee:

Notes & Bonds Trust Company
555 Main Street
City, State 00000
Facsimile: 777-777-6767

With a copy to (which copy shall not constitute notice):

[Notes & Bonds Trust Company's Counsel]
444 Smith Street
City, State 00000
Facsimile: 444-555-4545
Attention: John J. Doe, Esq.

ARTICLE 5

WAIVER AND AMENDMENT OF NOTICE PERIOD

Section 4.08. The Issuer hereby waives and dispense with the requirement in Section 7.08 of the Indenture that Resigning Trustee provide 30 days' notice to the Issuer of the resignation provided herein. The resignation of Resigning Trustee and appointment of Successor Trustee shall be effective as of the Effective Date.

IN WITNESS WHEREOF, the parties hereby have caused this Agreement to be duly executed as of the day and year first above written.

XYZ ISSUER CORP.
as Issuer

By:____
Name:
Title:

ABC CORPORATE TRUST COMPANY
As Resigning Trustee

By:____
Name:
Title:

NOTES & BONDS TRUST COMPANY
As Successor Trustee

By:____
Name:
Title:

SCHEDULE 1

DOCUMENTS TO BE DELIVERED TO SUCCESSOR TRUSTEE BY RESIGNING TRUSTEE

1. Executed copies of the Indenture, dated as of January 15, 2015, between the Issuer and Resigning Trustee and all amendments.
2. File of Closing Documents, which may be in electronic format (CD, DVD, PDF or other digital form).
3. A copy of the most recent SEC report delivered by the Issuer to Resigning Trustee pursuant to Section 4.03 of the Indenture.
4. A copy of the most recent Compliance Certificate delivered by the Issuer to Resigning Trustee pursuant to Section 4.03 of the Indenture.
5. Copies of any official notices sent by the Trustee to all the Holders of the Notes pursuant to the terms of the Indenture during the past 12 months and a copy of the most recent Trustee's annual report to Holders, if any.
6. Any and all Global Notes representing the Notes.

SCHEDULE 2

FORM OF NOTICE TO HOLDERS

[LETTERHEAD OF SUCCESSOR TRUSTEE]

To: The Holders of
10% Senior Notes due 2025 (CUSIP No.X123456789)[1] of XYZ Issuer Corp.

NOTICE IS HEREBY GIVEN, pursuant to Section 7.08 of the Indenture dated as of January 15, 2015, among XYZ Issuer Corp. as Issuer, ABC Corporate Trust Company, as Trustee, as amended and supplemented (the "Indenture"), that ABC Corporate Trust Company has resigned as Trustee, Registrar, Paying Agent and Custodian for the Global Notes under the Indenture.

Pursuant to Section 7.08 of the Indenture, Notes & Bonds Trust Company ("NBT") has accepted appointment as Trustee, Registrar, Paying Agent and Custodian for the Global Notes under the Indenture. The address of the Corporate Trust Office of NBT is 555 Main Street, City, State 00000.

The resignation by ABC Corporate Trust Company as Trustee and the appointment of NBT as successor Trustee became effective as of the opening of business on December 16, 2015.

Dated: December 16, 2015

Very truly yours,
Notes & Bonds Trust Company

[1] No representation is made as to the correctness of the CUSIP numbers either as printed on the Notes or as contained in this Notice.

APPENDIX B Direction Letter

[DATE]

ABC Corporate Trust Company
123 Smith Street
City, State 00000

Re: XYZ Issuer Corp.'s 10% Senior Notes due 2025 (the "Notes")

Ladies and Gentlemen:

Reference is made to the Indenture, dated January 15, 2015 (the "Indenture") by and between ABC Corporate Trust Company, N.A., as trustee (the "Trustee") and XYZ Issuer Corp. (the "Issuer"). All terms not otherwise defined in this letter shall have the respective meanings given to them in the Indenture.

Each of the undersigned is, as of the date hereof, the beneficial owner and/or investment advisor or manager of discretionary accounts for the beneficial owner of the aggregate principal amount of Notes set forth on its signature page (collectively, such beneficial owners are referred to as the "Directing Holders"). The Directing Holders collectively hold a majority of the aggregate outstanding principal amount of the Notes.

Pursuant to Section 6.05 of the Indenture, the Directing Holders hereby instruct the Trustee to [declare the principal of all the Notes and the interest accrued thereon to be due and payable immediately] (the "Instruction").

Pursuant to Section 6.05 of the Indenture, with respect to, and in connection with, any actions taken in accordance with and pursuant to the above Instruction, the undersigned Directing Holders each hereby agrees to, and shall, pay and reimburse and be liable jointly and severally to the Trustee and each director, officer and employee of the Trustee (the Trustee and each such other person being an "Indemnified Person") on demand for, and to indemnify and hold harmless each such Indemnified Person from and against, without limitation, any and all losses, liabilities, judgments, damages, claims, causes of actions, costs and expenses (including, for the avoidance of doubt, Trustee Counsel Fees and Expenses and Trustee Charges, as defined below) (collectively referred to herein as "Losses") incurred or suffered by an Indemnified Person, directly or indirectly, arising out of, related to, or connected with the compliance by the Trustee with the Instruction, or the taking or not taking of action in accordance with the Instruction, including, without limitation:

(i) any claim, cause of action, litigation, proceeding, action or investigation of any kind (whether civil, criminal or administrative, whether sounding in tort, contract or otherwise; whether such Indemnified Person is a party to claim, cause of action, litigation, proceeding, action or investigation; or whether brought by the Trustee, the Issuer, a holder or holders, or any other person) directly or indirectly arising from, related to, or in connection with, the taking or not taking by the Trustee or other Indemnified Person of action in accordance with this Instruction; or

(ii) Losses resulting from, arising out of or in any manner connected with, directly or indirectly, (a) a determination that the Trustee or any other Indemnified Person breached its or their duty under the Indenture as a result of relying upon and complying with the

Instruction, or (b) the enforcement of this letter; provided, however, that the foregoing indemnity (the "Indemnity") shall not be applicable to any Losses suffered or incurred by an Indemnified Person as a result of an Indemnified Person's gross negligence or willful misconduct as determined by a judgment of a court that is binding on such Indemnified Person, is final and is not subject to review on appeal.

Provided that this letter is executed on behalf of holders of a majority of the principal outstanding amount of the Notes, each of the undersigned hereby agrees that its obligations pursuant to this letter and the Indemnity contained herein shall be joint and several with each of the Directing Holders. This letter and the representations and warranties contained herein shall be binding upon each Directing Holder and its successors and assigns, provided however, that a Directing Holder shall not assign its obligations hereunder without the express written consent of the Trustee. This letter shall inure to the benefit of the Trustee and its successors and assigns.

Each of the undersigned Holders hereby represents and warrants that this letter and the Indemnity contained herein have been duly authorized, executed and delivered on its behalf and constitutes its legal, valid and binding obligations, enforceable in accordance with their respective terms, except as such enforceability may be limited by (i) bankruptcy, insolvency or other similar laws affecting creditors' rights generally and (ii) general principles of equity; and hereby waives any defenses based upon the invalidity of such representations and warranties.

The Trustee has retained [ABC's counsel] to represent it in connection with the actions to be taken pursuant to this Instruction and to represent it in connection with the Events of Default and the Trustee's duties under the Indenture. Each Holder hereby agrees to, and shall, pay and reimburse and be liable, jointly and severally, in accordance with each Holder's percentage ownership interest in the Notes for the attorneys' fees and expenses of [ABC's counsel] ("Trustee Counsel Fees and Expenses") incurred in connection with the Events of Default and actions taken pursuant to this Instruction (including, for the avoidance of doubt, fees and expenses incurred in connection with the preparation and execution of this direction letter), or otherwise in connection with the Trustee's duties under the Indenture, whether or not such fees and expenses have been paid by the Trustee. The Holders also recognize that the Trustee will bill for extraordinary time charges of the Trustee's internal personnel who render services in connection with the Instruction and the Events of Default ("Trustee Charges") and that such charges shall constitute Losses.

The undersigned Holders each agree that (a) the terms of this letter and the Indemnity contained herein shall be governed by and construed in accordance with the laws of the State of New York and (b) all actions and proceedings relating to or arising from, directly or indirectly, this letter and the Indemnity contained herein may be brought by any Indemnified Person in courts located in the Borough of Manhattan within the State of New York, and each of the undersigned Directing Holders hereby submits to personal jurisdiction of such courts for such actions or proceedings.

Each Directing Holder acknowledges and agrees that nothing contained in this letter agreement shall alter the rights and obligations of the Trustee under the Indenture, including, without limitation, the right of the Trustee under Section 6.05 of the Indenture to refuse to follow certain directions, including, without limitation, directions that conflict with law or the Indenture.

Any Directing Holder may sell some or all of its Notes to another party and permit the buying party to become a Directing Holder under this letter agreement on the same terms and conditions as all other

Directing Holders. Such transfer shall not, however, release any such Directing Holder from its obligations or liabilities hereunder without the express written consent of the Trustee with respect thereto.

This letter may be executed by each Directing Holder in separate counterparts and the Trustee is hereby instructed to accept the signature pages of such counterparts.

APPENDIX C Notice of Event of Default and Filing of Chapter 11 Case

TO THE HOLDERS OF:
XYZ ISSUER CORP. (the "Company")
10% SENIOR NOTES DUE 2025
(CUSIP NO. X123456789)* (the "Notes")

* The CUSIP numbers are included herein solely for the convenience of the registered owners of the Notes. No representation is made as to the correctness or accuracy of the CUSIP numbers either as printed on the Notes or as contained in this Notice.

THIS NOTICE CONTAINS IMPORTANT INFORMATION THAT IS OF INTEREST TO THE REGISTERED AND BENEFICIAL OWNERS OF THE NOTES. ALL DEPOSITORIES, BROKERS, CUSTODIANS, AND OTHER INTERMEDIARIES RECEIVING THIS NOTICE ARE REQUESTED TO EXPEDITE RE-TRANSMITTAL TO BENEFICIAL OWNERS OF THE NOTES IN A TIMELY MANNER.

Notes & Bonds Trust Company ("NBT"), as successor trustee (the "Trustee") pursuant to that certain Agreement of Resignation, Appointment and Acceptance dated as of December 15, 2015, among the ABC Corporate Trust Company, as resigning trustee (the "Resigning Trustee"), and NBT, and as the Trustee under that certain Indenture dated as of January 15, 2015, as amended and supplemented (the "Indenture"), hereby gives this notice to the holders of the Notes. Unless otherwise noted, capitalized terms used but not defined herein shall have the meaning given them in the Indenture.

Chapter 11 Filing

On January 15, 2016, the Company and certain subsidiaries and affiliates filed petitions under chapter 11 of the Federal Bankruptcy Code in the United States Bankruptcy Court for the Southern District of New York, (the "Court") commencing cases jointly administered under the caption *In re XYZ Issuer Corp.* Case No. 16-00000 (the "Case"). The Company's chapter 11 filing constitutes an Event of Default under Section 6.01 of the Indenture.

Information regarding the Case is available to the public without charge on the website of the Company's claims and noticing agent at the following link: [http://link.com/link/].

Direction to the Trustee

Section 6.05 of the Indenture provides that holders of a majority in principal amount of outstanding Notes of each series may direct the Trustee as to the time, method and place of conducting any proceeding for any remedy available to the Trustee or of exercising any trust or power conferred on the Trustee. The holders' ability to direct the Trustee is subject to the requirements of Section 7.02 of the Indenture, which, among other things, states that the holders must provide the Trustee with security or indemnity satisfactory to the Trustee against costs, expenses and liabilities which might be incurred as a result of the Trustee's compliance with the holders' direction before the Trustee complies with the direction.

Retention of Professionals

The Trustee has retained the law firm of [Trustee Law Firm] to represent the Trustee in connection with the Indenture, the Notes and the Case. The firm's address is [444 Smith Street, City, State 00000.

Trustee's Fees and Expenses

NBT in its capacity as Trustee for the Notes has incurred and will continue to incur fees, expenses and disbursements, including professional fees, expenses and disbursements, from time to time. NBT reserves its rights under Section 7.07 of the Indenture for reimbursement of any of its unpaid fees and expenses, including the Trustee's professional fees, expenses and disbursements, prior to payment of the Notes.

Future Events

The Trustee may periodically communicate with holders of the Notes through written notice of material events of a public nature of which the Trustee has knowledge. While the Trustee will endeavor to keep you informed of major developments that affect your Notes, the Trustee does not intend to provide you with regular updates.

Communications to the Trustee

The Trustee will continue to communicate with holders with respect to any potential future distributions to holders or as circumstances may otherwise warrant. If you wish to contact the Trustee regarding the Notes or the contents of this notice, we ask that you do so in writing directed to: info@indenturetrustee.nyc.

The Trustee may conclude that a specific response to specific inquiries from particular holders may not be appropriate either because the disclosure in question may not be in the best interest of all holders or may not be consistent with the equal and full dissemination of information to all holders.

Holders should not rely on the Trustee as their sole source of information. The Trustee makes no recommendations and gives no investment, legal, tax or other advice as to the above matters or as to the Notes generally.

NOTES & BONDS TRUST COMPANY, as Trustee
[DATE]

APPENDIX D Notice of Bar Date for Filing of Proofs of Claim

TO THE HOLDERS OF:
XYZ ISSUER CORP. (the "Company")
10% SENIOR NOTES DUE 2025
(CUSIP NO. X123456789)* (the "Notes")

* The CUSIP numbers are included herein solely for the convenience of the registered owners of the Notes. No representation is made as to the correctness or accuracy of the CUSIP numbers either as printed on the Notes or as contained in this Notice.

THIS NOTICE CONTAINS IMPORTANT INFORMATION THAT IS OF INTEREST TO THE REGISTERED AND BENEFICIAL OWNERS OF THE NOTES. ALL DEPOSITORIES, BROKERS, CUSTODIANS, AND OTHER INTERMEDIARIES RECEIVING THIS NOTICE ARE REQUESTED TO EXPEDITE RE-TRANSMITTAL TO BENEFICIAL OWNERS OF THE NOTES IN A TIMELY MANNER.

Notes & Bonds Trust Company ("NBT"), as successor trustee (the "Trustee") pursuant to that certain Agreement of Resignation, Appointment and Acceptance dated as of December 15, 2015 among the ABC Corporate Trust Company, as resigning trustee (the "Resigning Trustee"), and NBT, and as the Trustee under that certain Indenture dated as of January 15, 2015, as amended and supplemented (the "Indenture"), hereby gives this notice to the holders of the Notes. Unless otherwise noted, capitalized terms used but not defined herein shall have the meaning given them in the Indenture.

Chapter 11 Case

As you were previously notified, on January 15, 2016, the Company and certain subsidiaries and affiliates filed petitions under chapter 11 of the Federal Bankruptcy Code in the United States Bankruptcy Court for the Southern District of New York, (the "Court") commencing cases jointly administered under the caption *In re XYZ Issuer Corp.* Case No. 16-00000 (the "Case").

Information regarding the Case is available to the public without charge on the website of the Company's claims and noticing agent at the following link: [http://link.com/link/].

Proofs of Claim

The Court has established June 15, 2016 as the bar date for filing proofs of claim on account of prepetition debt by non-governmental entities. On behalf of itself and the Holders, the Trustee will file timely a proof of claim for all obligations due under the Indenture. Consequently, it is unnecessary for individual Holders to file proofs of claim with respect to the Notes.

Direction to the Trustee

Section 6.05 of the Indenture provides that holders of a majority in principal amount of outstanding Notes of each series may direct the Trustee as to the time, method and place of conducting any proceeding for any remedy available to the Trustee or of exercising any trust or power conferred on the Trustee. The holders' ability to direct the Trustee is subject to the requirements of Section 7.02 of the Indenture, which, among other things, states that the holders must provide the Trustee with security or indemnity satisfactory to the Trustee against costs, expenses and liabilities which might be incurred as a result of the Trustee's compliance with the holders' direction before the Trustee complies with the direction.

Retention of Professionals

The Trustee has retained the law firm of [Trustee Law Firm] to represent the Trustee in connection with the Indenture, the Notes and the Case. The firm's address is [444 Smith Street, City, State 00000.

Trustee's Fees and Expenses

NBT in its capacity as Trustee for the Notes has incurred and will continue to incur fees, expenses and disbursements, including professional fees, expenses and disbursements, from time to time. NBT reserves its rights under Section 7.07 of the Indenture for reimbursement of any of its unpaid fees and expenses, including the Trustee's professional fees, expenses and disbursements, prior to payment of the Notes.

Future Events

The Trustee may periodically communicate with holders of the Notes through written notice of material events of a public nature of which the Trustee has knowledge. While the Trustee will endeavor to keep you informed of major developments that affect your Notes, the Trustee does not intend to provide you with regular updates.

Communications to the Trustee

The Trustee will continue to communicate with holders with respect to any potential future distributions to holders or as circumstances may otherwise warrant. If you wish to contact the Trustee regarding the Notes or the contents of this notice, we ask that you do so in writing directed to: info@indenturetrustee.nyc.

The Trustee may conclude that a specific response to specific inquiries from particular holders may not be appropriate either because the disclosure in question may not be in the best interest of all holders or may not be consistent with the equal and full dissemination of information to all holders.

Holders should not rely on the Trustee as their sole source of information. The Trustee makes no recommendations and gives no investment, legal, tax or other advice as to the above matters or as to the Notes generally.

NOTES & BONDS TRUST COMPANY, as Trustee
[DATE]

APPENDIX E Notice of Filing of Plan and Disclosure Statement

TO THE HOLDERS OF:
XYZ ISSUER CORP. (the "Company")
10% SENIOR NOTES DUE 2025
(CUSIP NO. X123456789)* (the "Notes")

THIS NOTICE CONTAINS IMPORTANT INFORMATION THAT IS OF INTEREST TO THE REGISTERED AND BENEFICIAL OWNERS OF THE NOTES. ALL DEPOSITORIES, BROKERS, CUSTODIANS, AND OTHER INTERMEDIARIES RECEIVING THIS NOTICE ARE REQUESTED TO EXPEDITE RE-TRANSMITTAL TO BENEFICIAL OWNERS OF THE NOTES IN A TIMELY MANNER.

*No representation is made as to the correctness of the CUSIP numbers either as printed on the Notes or as contained in this Notice.

Notes & Bonds Trust Company ("NBT") as trustee (the "Trustee") pursuant to that certain Agreement of Resignation, Appointment and Acceptance dated as of December 15, 2015 by and among the Company, ABC Corporate Trust Company, as resigning trustee (the "Resigning Trustee"), and NBT, and as the Trustee under that certain Indenture dated as of January 1, 2015, as amended and supplemented (the "Indenture"), among the Company and the Resigning Trustee, hereby gives this notice to the holders of the Notes. Unless otherwise noted, capitalized terms used but not defined herein shall have the meaning given them in the Indenture.

Chapter 11 Case

As indicated in the Trustee's prior notice dated [DATE] the Company and certain of its affiliates (collectively, the "Debtors") filed voluntary petitions for relief under chapter 11 of the United States Bankruptcy Code (the "Case") in the United States Bankruptcy Court for the Southern District of New York (the "Court") on January 15, 2016. The Case is jointly administered pursuant to an order of the Bankruptcy Court under main case no. 16-00000.

Filing of Proofs of Claim

On behalf of itself and the Holders, on June 1, 2016, the Trustee submitted proofs of claim against the Company in the total amount of principal due on account of the Notes at the time of the filing of the Case ($1,000,000,000), plus accrued interest, costs and expenses of the Trustee and its professionals and all other obligations arising under the Notes and Indenture.

Filing of Plan of Reorganization and Related Disclosure Statements

On [DATE], 2016, the Debtors filed a Chapter 11 Plan of Reorganization [Docket # XXY] and accompanying Disclosure Statement [Docket # XXXY] The Debtors filed a motion for entry of an order scheduling certain hearing dates and deadlines and establishing certain protocols in connection with the confirmation of Debtor's Plan of Reorganization and the Approval of Debtor's Disclosure Statement (the "Scheduling Motion") [Docket # XYXY]. A hearing on the Scheduling Motion was held on [DATE] at [TIME] a.m. before the Court, at which the Court granted the scheduling motion. On [DATE], the Bankruptcy Court entered the Order (A) Scheduling Certain Hearing Dates and Deadlines, (B) Establishing

Certain Protocols in Connection with the Approval of Debtors' Disclosure Statement, and (C) Establishing the Terms Governing Mediation (the "Scheduling Order") [Docket # XXYY]. The Scheduling Order sets dates and procedures pertaining to approval of the Debtors' Disclosure Statement, including the following dates governing Disclosure Statement objections (all times are prevailing Eastern Time):

- Objections to Disclosure Statement must be filed by [DATE]
- Debtors' reply to objections to Disclosure Statement must be filed by [DATE] **at 4:00 PM**.
- Disclosure Statement Hearing commences on [DATE] **at 10:00 AM**.

This following summary of the Plan is provided for your convenience only. The Debtors' plan classifies the claims of holders of Notes (the "Notes Claims") in Class 4 as impaired and entitled to vote. The Plan treatment of Class 4 is as follows:

> The Notes Claims will receive a cash distribution equal to 50% of the allowed amount of outstanding principal (but without any accrued interest, premium, fees, or any other obligations), in cash on the Plan effective date.

Holders should review the Plan, the Disclosure Statement, and the information provided by the Debtors' claims agent, including documents and pleadings filed with the Court, available at the following link http://link.link.link.com/link.

The Trustee does not have the right to vote on the Plan, and the Trustee makes no recommendation with respect to the Plan.

Retention of Professionals

As indicated in the Trustee's prior Notice dated [DATE], the Trustee has retained the law firm of Bryan Cave LLP ("Bryan Cave") and specifically Stephanie Wickouski to represent the Trustee in connection with the Indenture, the Notes and the Case. The firm's address is Bryan Cave LLP, 1290 Avenue of the Americas, 35th Floor, New York, New York, 10104, Phone (212) 541-1114.

Direction to the Trustee

Section 6.05 of the Indenture provides that Holders of a majority in principal amount of outstanding Notes may direct the Trustee as to the time, method and place of conducting any proceeding for any remedy available to the Trustee or exercising any trust or power conferred on the Trustee. The Holders' ability to direct the Trustee is subject to the requirements of Section 7.01(e) of the Indenture, which, among other things, state that the Holders must provide the Trustee with satisfactory indemnity against loss, liabilities or expense which might be incurred as a result of the Holders' requests before the Trustee need follow the direction of the Holders.

Trustee's Fees and Expenses

NBT in its capacity as Trustee for the Notes has incurred and will continue to incur fees, expenses and disbursements, including professional fees, expenses and disbursements, from time to time. The Trustee reserves its rights under Section 7.07 of the Indenture for reimbursement of any of its unpaid fees and expenses, including Trustee's professional fees, expenses and disbursements, prior to payment of the Notes.

Future Events

The Trustee may periodically communicate with Holders through written notice of material events of a public nature of which the Trustee has knowledge. While the Trustee will endeavor to keep you informed of major developments that affect your Notes, the Trustee does not intend to provide you with regular updates of the Court proceedings. Updates to the Bankruptcy Court docket in this proceeding are available through the Company's claims and noticing agent.

Communications to the Trustee

If you wish to contact the Trustee regarding the Notes or the contents of this notice, we ask that you do so in writing directed to: info@indenturetrustee.nyc.

The Trustee has prepared this communication based upon information supplied to it without independent investigation.

This notice is being given without prejudice to any rights or remedies which may be available to the Trustee or to any Holders, all of which are expressly reserved. Holders should not rely on the Trustee as their sole source of information.

The Trustee makes no recommendations and gives no investment, legal, tax or other advice as to the above matters or as to the Notes generally.

NOTES & BONDS TRUST COMPANY, as Trustee

[DATE]

Table of Authorities

Cases

In re 203 N. LaSalle St. Partnership, 246 B.R. 325 (Bankr. N.D. Ill. 2000)

Adams v. Zimmerman, 73 F.3d 1164 (1st Cir. 1996)

In re Adelphia Communications Corp., No. 02-41729, J. Gerber (Bankr. S.D.N.Y. April 6, 2006)

In re Adelphia Communications Corp., 359 B.R. 54, 63 (Bankr. S.D.N.Y. 2006)

In re Adelphia Communications Corp., 441 B.R. 6 (Bankr. S.D.N.Y. 2010)

AG Capital Funding Partners, L.P. v. State St. Bank & Trust Co., 11 N.Y.3d 146, 866 N.Y.S.2d 578 (2008)

Akanthos Capital Mgmt., LLC v. CompuCredit Holdings Corp., 677 F.3d 1286 (11th Cir. 2012)

In re American Roads LLC, 496 B.R. 727 (Bankr. S.D.N.Y. 2013)

In re AMR Corp., 485 B.R. 279 (Bankr. S.D.N.Y.), *aff'd*, 730 F.3d 88 (2d Cir. 2013), *cert. denied*, 134 S. Ct. 1888 (2014)

In re AMR Corp., 730 F.3d 88 (2d Cir. 2013)

Beck v. Manufacturers Hanover Trust Co., 218 A.D.2d 1, 632 N.Y.S.2d 520 (1st Dep't 1995)

Bluebird Partners, L.P. v. First Fidelity Bank, N.A. N.J., 85 F.3d 970 (2d Cir. 1996)

Bluebird Partners, L.P. v. Bank of New York, Index No.: 601016/96, 2010 N.Y. Misc. LEXIS 2503 (Sup. Ct. N.Y. Cnty. June 7, 2010)

BNP Paribas Mortg. Corp. v. Bank of America, N.A., 778 F. Supp. 2d 375 (S.D.N.Y. 2011)

Caplin v. Marine Midland Grace Trust Co. of N.Y., 406 U.S. 416 (1972)

Central Bank of Denver N.A. v. Deloitte & Touche, 928 P.2d 754 (Colo. Ct. App. 1996)

In re Central Medical Center, Inc., 122 B.R. 568 (Bankr. E.D. Mo. 1990)

In re Chemtura Corp., 439 B.R. 561 (Bankr. S.D.N.Y. 2010)

Chesapeake Energy Corp. v. Bank of N.Y. Mellon Trust Co., N.A., 773 F.3d 110 (2d Cir. 2014)

Class Five Nev. Claimants v. Dow Corning Corp. (In re Dow Corning Corp.), 280 F.3d 648 (6th Cir. 2002)

In re Continental Airlines, 203 F.3d 203 (3d Cir. 2000)

Cort v. Ash, 422 U.S. 66 (1975)

Cortlandt St. Recovery Corp. v Hellas Telecomms., S.a.r.l., 47 Misc. 3d 544, 996 N.Y.S.2d 476 (Sup. Ct. N.Y. Cnty. 2014)

Crosby v. Nat'l Foreign Trade Council, 530 U.S. 363 (2000)

Cruden v. Bank of N.Y., 957 F.2d 961 (2d Cir. 1992)

Dabney v. Chase Nat'l Bank of City of N.Y., 196 F.2d 668 (2d Cir. 1952), *opinion supplemented by*, 201 F.2d 635 (2d Cir. 1953)

In re Dana Corp., 390 B.R. 100 (Bankr. S.D.N.Y. 2008)

Davis v. Elliot Mgmt. Corp. (In re Lehman Bros. Holdings Inc.), 508 B.R. 283 (S.D.N.Y. 2014)

Davis v. Elliot Mgmt. Corp. (In re Lehman Bros. Holdings Inc.), No. 13 Civ. 2211(RJS), 2014 WL 3408574 (S.D.N.Y. June 30, 2014)

In re Delta Airlines, Inc., 370 B.R. 537 (Bankr. S.D.N.Y. 2007), *aff'd*, 374 B.R. 516 (S.D.N.Y 2007), *aff'd*, 309 Fed. App'x 455 (2d Cir. 2009)

In re Dura Automotive Systems, Inc., 379 B.R. 257 (Bankr. D. Del. 2007)

In re E.F. Hutton Southwest Properties II, Ltd. 953 F.2d. 963 (5th Cir. 1992)

Ellington Credit Fund, Ltd. V. Select Portfolio Servicing, Inc., 837 F. Supp. 2d 162 (S.D.N.Y. 2011)

In re Equity Funding Corp. of Am. Sec. Litig., 416 F. Supp. 161 (C.D. Cal. 1976), *aff'd*, 603 F.2d 1353 (9th Cir. 1979)

In re Enron Corp. Sec., Derivative & "ERISA" Litig., No. MDL-1446, Civ. Action Nos. H-01-3624, 03-5808, 2008 WL 744823 (S.D. Tex. Mar. 19, 2008)

In re Envirodyne Indus., Inc., 161 B.R. 440 (Bankr. N.D. Ill. 1993), *aff'd,* 29 F.3d 301 (7th Cir. 1994)

In re Envirodyne Indus., Inc., 174 B.R. 986 (Bankr. N.D. Ill. 1994)

Excelsior Fund, Inc. v. JP Morgan Chase Bank, N.A., 06 Civ. 5246 (JGK), 2007 U.S. Dist. LEXIS 22966 (S.D.N.Y. Mar. 22, 2007)

In re Global Power Equipment Group Inc., Nos. 06-11045(BLS), 1911, 2191, 2213, 2008 WL 435197 (Bankr. D. Del., Feb. 14, 2008), *aff'd,* 400 B.R. 17 (D. Del. 2009)

Hall Fin. Group, Inc. v. DP Partners Ltd. P'ship (Matter of DP Partners Ltd. P'ship.), 106 F.3d 667 (5th Cir. 1997)

Haskins v. U.S. (In re Lister), 846 F.2d 55 (10th Cir. 1988)

Hildene Capital Mgmt., LLC v. The Bank of New York Mellon, Index No. 650980/10, J. O. Peter Sherwood (Sup. Ct. N.Y. Cnty. Jan. 5, 2015)

Hooper Assocs. V. AGS Computers, 74 N.Y.2d 487, 549 N.Y.S.2d 365 (1989)

HSBC Bank USA, N.A. v. Calpine Corp., No. 07 Civ 3088 (GBD), 2010 WL 3835200 (S.D.N.Y. Sept. 15, 2010)

In re Innkeepers USA Trust, 448 B.R. 131 (Bankr. S.D.N.Y. 2011)

Kusner v. First Pennsylvania Corp., 531 F.2d 1234 (3d Cir. 1976)

Lebron v. Mechem Fin. Inc., 27 F.3d 937 (3d Cir. 1994)

In re Lehman Brothers Holdings Inc., 487 B.R 181 (Bankr. S.D.N.Y. 2013)

LaSalle Nat'l Bank v. Perelman, 141 F. Supp. 2d 451 (D. Del. 2001)

LTV Corp. v. Valley Fidelity Bank & Trust Co. (In re Chateaugay Corp.), 961 F.2d 378 (2d Cir. 1992)

Marblegate Asset Mgmt., LLC v. Education Mgmt. Corp., No. 14 Civ. 8584 (KPF), 2015 WL 3867643 (S.D.N.Y. June 23, 2015)

In re Manville Forest Prods. Corp., 43 B.R 293 (Bankr. S.D.N.Y. 1984), *aff'd in part, rev'd in part,* 60 B.R. 403 (S.D.N.Y. 1986)

Martin v. Bank of Germantown (In re Martin), 761 F.2d 1163 (6th Cir. 1985)

McMahan & Co. v. Wherehouse Entm't, Inc., 859 F. Supp. 743 (S.D.N.Y. 1994), *aff'd in part, rev'd in part*, 65 F.3d 1044 (2d Cir. 1995)

MeehanCombs Global Credit Opportunities Funds, L.P. v. Caesars Entm't Corp., Nos. 14-cv-7091 (SAS), 14-cv-7973 (SAS), 2015 WL 221055 (S.D.N.Y. Jan. 15, 2015)

In re Metromedia Fiber Network, Inc., 416 F.3d 136 (2d Cir. 2005).

Morris v. Cantor, 390 F. Supp. 817 (S.D.N.Y. 1975)

In re MPM Silicones, LLC, Case No. 14-22503 rrd, 2014 WL 4436335 (Bankr. S.D.N.Y. Sept. 9, 2014)

In re MPM Silicones, LLC, 531 B.R. 321 (S.D.N.Y. 2015)

Nationsbank, N.A. v. McGraw-Hill Cos., Civil Action No. H-94-0882, 1996 U.S. Dist. LEXIS 22414 (S.D. Tex. Dec. 12, 1996)

N.I.S. Corp. v. Hallahan (Matter of Hallahan), 936 F.2d 1496 (7th Cir. 1991)

Ogle v. Fidelity & Deposit Co. of Maryland, 586 F.3d 143 (2d Cir. 2009)

In re Premier Entm't Biloxi LLC, 445 B.R. 582 (Bankr. S.D. Miss. 2010)

In re PWS Holding Corp., 228 F.3d 224 (3d Cir. 2000)

Quadrant Structured Prods. Co., Ltd. v. Vertin, 23 N.Y.3d 549, 992 N.Y.S.2d 687 (2014)

In re Quebecor World (USA) Inc., 719 F.3d 94 (2d Cir. 2013)

RBC Capital Markets, LLC v. Education Loan Trust IV, Civ. Action No. 6297-CS, 2011 WL 6152282 (Del. Ch. Dec. 6, 2011)

Regions Bank v. Blount Parrish & Co., Inc., No. 01CV0031, 2001 WL 726989 (N.D. Ill., June 27, 2001)

In re Residential Capital, LLC, 501 B.R. 549 (Bankr. S.D.N.Y. 2013)

Royal Park Investments SA/NV v. HSBC Bank USA, N.A., Nos. 14-cv-8175(SAS), 14-cv-9366(SAS), 14-cv-10101(SAS), 2015 WL 3466121 (S.D.N.Y. June 1, 2015)

Schmidt v. Rodriguez (In re Rodriguez), No. 10-70606, 2013 WL 2450925 (Bankr. S.D. Tex. June 5, 2013)

In re School Specialty, Inc., No. 13-10125 (KJC), 2013 WL 1838513 (Bankr. D. Del. April 22, 2013)

SE Property Holdings, LLC v. Seaside Engineering & Surveying, Inc. (In re Seaside Engineering & Surveying, Inc.), No. 14-11590, J. Anderson (11th Cir. Mar. 12, 2015)

In re SNTL Corp., 571 F.3d 826 (9th Cir. 2009)

In re Solutia Inc., 379 B.R. 473 (Bankr. S.D.N.Y. 2007)

Speights & Runyan v. Celotex Corp. (In re Celotex Corp.), 227 F.3d 1336 (11th Cir. 2000)

In re Summit Metals, Inc., 379 B.R. 40 (Bankr. D. Del. 2007), *aff'd,* 406 Fed. App'x 634 (3d Cir. 2011)

Taylor v. U.S. Bank, N.A., CIVIL ACTION H-12-3550, 2015 U.S. Dist. LEXIS 14194 (S.D. Tex. Feb. 6, 2015)

Travelers Cas. & Sur. Co. of America v. Pacific Gas & Elec. Co., 549 U.S. 443 (2007)

In re Trico Marine Servs., Inc., 450 B.R. 474 (Bankr. D. Del. 2011)

Upic & Co. v. Kinder-Care Learning Ctrs., Inc., 793 F. Supp. 448 (S.D.N.Y. 1992)

U.S. Bank Nat'l Ass'n v. U.S. Timberlands Klamath Falls, L.L.C., No. Civ.A. 112-N, 2004 WL 1699057 (Del.Ch. July 29, 2004)

United States Trust Co. of N.Y. v. First Nat'l City Bank, 57 A.D. 2d 285, 394 N.Y.S.2d 653 (1st Dept. 1977), *aff'd,* 45 N.Y.2d 869, 410 N.Y.S.2d 580 (1978)

U.S. Trust Co. of N.Y. v. LTV Steel Co. (In re Chateaugay Corp.), 150 B.R. 529 (Bankr. S.D.N.Y. 1993), *aff'd,* 170 B.R. 551 (S.D.N.Y. 1994)

Victor v. Riklis, No. 91 Civ. 2897 (LJF), 1992 WL 122911 (S.D.N.Y. May 15, 1992)

In re Washington Mutual, Inc. 442 B.R. 314 (Bankr. D. Del. 2011)

In re Washington Pub. Power Supply Sys. Sec. Litig., 623 F. Supp. 1466 (D Wash. 1985), *aff'd,* 823 F.2d 1349 (9th Cir. 1987)

In re Waterman, 248 B.R. 567 (8th Cir. BAP 2000)

Welsbach Elec. Corp. v. MasTec N. Am., Inc., 7 N.Y.3d 624, 825 N.Y.S.2d 692 (2006)

In re Worldwide Direct, Inc., 334 B.R. 112 (Bankr. D. Del 2005)

In re W.R. Grace & Co., 475 B.R. 34 (D. Del. 2012), *aff'd*, 729 F.3d 332 (3d Cir. 2013)

Zeffiro v. First Pennsylvania Banking and Trust Co., 623 F.2d 290 (3d Cir. 1980)

Statutes & Other Authorities

11 U.S.C. § 101(5)(A)

11 U.S.C. § 365

11 U.S.C. § 501(a)

11 U.S.C. §§ 502(a), (b), (b)(2)

11 U.S.C. § 503(b)(3)(F)

11 U.S.C. §§ 506(b), (c)

11 U.S.C. § 510

11 U.S.C. § 544

11 U.S.C. § 546(e)

11 U.S.C. § 548

11 U.S.C. §§ 1102(a), (b)(1)

11 U.S.C. §§ 1109(a), (b)

11 U.S.C. § 1112

11 U.S.C. § 1123(a)(5)(F)

11 U.S.C. § 1124(2)

11 U.S.C. §§ 1122-1129

15 U.S.C. §§ 77a-77aa

15 U.S.C. §§ 77aaa-77bbbb

15 U.S.C. § 306

15 U.S.C. § 310(b)(1)

15 U.S.C. § 310(b)(10)

15 U.S.C. §§ 315(a)-(d)

15 U.S.C. § 316(b)

15 U.S.C. §§ 317(a), (a)(1)-(2)

15 U.S.C. § 318(c)

28 U.S.C. § 151
28 U.S.C. § 156(c)
28 U.S.C. §§ 1452(a), (b)
Fed. R. Bankr. P. 3001(a), (b), (c)(1), (d)
Fed. R. Bankr. P. 3002(b)(5), (d), (e)
Fed. R. Bankr. P. 3003(c)(5), (d)
Fed. R. Bankr. P. 3007(b)
Fed. R. Bankr. P. 3017(d), (e)
Fed. R. Bankr. P. 5005
Fed. R. Bankr. P. 9027(a)(1), (d)
17 C.F.R. § 230.501
17 C.F.R. § 243.100
N.Y. Gen Oblig. § 5-1401
The ABA Revised Simplified Model Indenture and Commentary, 53 Bus. Law 1115 (2000)
Model Indenture § 6.01
Model Indenture § 6.03
Model Indenture § 6.05
Model Indenture § 6.06
Model Indenture § 6.07
Model Indenture § 6.08
Model Indenture § 6.10
Model Indenture § 6.11
Model Indenture §§ 7.01(a), (b)(2), (c)(2), (c)(3), (c)(4)
Model Indenture § 7.02(b)
Model Indenture § 7.07
Model Indenture § 7.08
Model Indenture § 11.12
Model Indenture § 11.13
Subordinated Notes Indenture § 1.01

Harold L. Kaplan & Mark F. Hebbeln, The Anglo-American Indenture—Covenant Enforcement and Bond Defaults—U.S. Experience and Lessons from Canada and the U.K., A.B.A. SEC. BUS. LAW 1, 4 (Spring 2009), available at: http://www.abanet.org/buslaw/newsletter/0081/materials/pp1.pdf; Steven L. Schwarcz, Fiduciaries with Conflicting Obligations, available at: http://scholarship.law.duke.edu/cgi/viewcontent.cgi?article=2757&context=faculty_scholarship

www.ingramcontent.com/pod-product-compliance
Ingram Content Group UK Ltd.
Pitfield, Milton Keynes, MK11 3LW, UK
UKHW020800290926
15470UKWH00008B/1837/J

9 781587 983054